Return to Riemann

This book is a music-theoretical and critical-theoretical study of late tonal music, and, in particular, of the music of Wagner's *Götterdämmerung*.

First, in terms of music theory, it proposes a new theory of tonal function that returns to the theories of Hugo Riemann to rediscover a development of his thought that has been covered over by the recent project of neo-Riemannian theory. Second, in terms of its philosophical approach, it reawakens the critical-theoretical examination of the relation between music and the late capitalist society that is sedimented in the musical materials themselves, and which the music, in turn, subjects to aesthetically embodied critique. The music, the theory, and the listeners and critics who respond to them are all radically reimagined.

This book will be of interest to professional music theorists, undergraduates, and technically inclined musicians and listeners, that is, anyone who is fascinated by the chromatic magic of late-nineteenth-century music.

J. P. E. Harper-Scott is Emeritus Professor of Music History and Theory at Royal Holloway, University of London, UK. He is the author of numerous books and articles, including *The Event of Music History*, *Ideology in Britten's Operas*, *The Quilting Points of Musical Modernism*, and *Edward Elgar, Modernist*.

Oliver Chandler is an Academic Professor at the Royal College of Music and stipendiary lecturer in music at Keble and Hertford Colleges, University of Oxford, UK. He is the author of *A Twelve-Tone Repertory for Guitar: Julian Bream and the British Serialists, 1956–1983*.

Royal Musical Association Monographs
Series Editor: Catherine A. Bradley

This series was originally supported by funds made available to the Royal Musical Association from the estate of Thurston Dart, former King Edward Professor of Music at the University of London. The editorial board is the Publications Committee of the Association.

No. 34: The Pre-History of The Midsummer Marriage Narratives and Speculations: Narratives and Speculations
Roger Savage

No. 35: Felice Giardini and Professional Music Culture in Mid-Eighteenth-Century London
Cheryll Duncan

No. 36: Disinformation in Mass Media: Gluck, Piccinni and the Journal de Paris
Beverly Jerold

No. 37: Music Theory in Late Medieval Avignon: Magister Johannes Pipardi
Karen M. Cook

No. 38: Gregorio Ballabene's Forty-eight-part Mass for Twelve Choirs (1772)
Florian Bassani

No. 39: Authorship and Identity in Late Thirteenth-Century Motets
Catherine A. Bradley

No. 40: The Malmariée in the Thirteenth-Century Motet
Dolores Pesce

No. 41: Music, Books and Theatre in Eighteenth-Century Exton: A Context for Handel's 'Comus'
Colin Timms

No. 42: Return to Riemann: Tonal Function and Chromatic Music
J. P. E. Harper-Scott and Oliver Chandler

For more information about this series, please visit: www.routledge.com/music/series/RMA

Return to Riemann
Tonal Function and Chromatic Music

**J. P. E. Harper-Scott and
Oliver Chandler**

LONDON AND NEW YORK

First published 2024
by Routledge
4 Park Square, Milton Park, Abingdon, Oxon OX14 4RN

and by Routledge
605 Third Avenue, New York, NY 10158

Routledge is an imprint of the Taylor & Francis Group, an informa business

© 2024 J. P. E. Harper-Scott and Oliver Chandler

The right of J. P. E. Harper-Scott and Oliver Chandler to be identified as authors of this work has been asserted in accordance with sections 77 and 78 of the Copyright, Designs and Patents Act 1988.

All rights reserved. No part of this book may be reprinted or reproduced or utilised in any form or by any electronic, mechanical, or other means, now known or hereafter invented, including photocopying and recording, or in any information storage or retrieval system, without permission in writing from the publishers.

Trademark notice: Product or corporate names may be trademarks or registered trademarks, and are used only for identification and explanation without intent to infringe.

British Library Cataloguing-in-Publication Data
A catalogue record for this book is available from the British Library

Library of Congress Cataloging-in-Publication Data
Names: Harper-Scott, J. P. E. (John Paul Edward), 1977- author. | Chandler, Oliver, author.
Title: Return to Riemann: tonal function and chromatic music/ J. P. E. Harper-Scott and Oliver Chandler.
Description: [First edition.] | Abingdon, Oxon; New York: Routledge, 2024. | Series: Royal Musical Association monographs | Includes bibliographical references and index.
Identifiers: LCCN 2023047568 (print) | LCCN 2023047569 (ebook) | ISBN 9781032025056 (hardback) | ISBN 9781032025063 (paperback) | ISBN 9781003183655 (ebook)
Subjects: LCSH: Music–19th century–Analysis, appreciation. | Tonality. | Chromaticism (Music) | Riemann, Hugo, 1849-1919–Criticism and interpretation.
Classification: LCC MT90 .H38 2024 (print) | LCC MT90 (ebook) | DDC 780.9/034–dceng/20231027
LC record available at https://lccn.loc.gov/2023047568
LC ebook record available at https://lccn.loc.gov/2023047569

ISBN: 9781032025056 (hbk)
ISBN: 9781032025063 (pbk)
ISBN: 9781003183655 (ebk)

DOI: 10.4324/9781003183655

Typeset in Times New Roman
by Deanta Global Publishing Services, Chennai, India

To Diana, for two decades of persevering through the sour and uncouth dissonances

Contents

	Acknowledgements	*viii*
	Introduction	1
1	Riemannian Theory and the Problem of Chromatic Function	7
2	Waltraute's Plaint: Riemannian Tonal Function and Dramatic Narrative	26
3	Two Nineteenth-Century Examples of Hexatonic-Diatonic Tonal Function	41
4	The Multiple Lives of Seventh Chords	56
5	'Here Time Becomes Space': Schenkerising Riemann/ Riemannising Schenker	74
	Glossary of Riemannian Symbology	*87*
	Index	*89*

Acknowledgements

The authors would like to thank Simon Keefe and Heidi Bishop for their faith in this project. Without it, this book may never have come into being.

OC would like to thank Paul for encouraging him to return to Riemann, and his students at the University of Oxford and Royal Holloway, University of London, on whom much of the material in this book was workshopped; Izzie Thorneycroft, Patrick Renehan, Jake Sternberg, and Douggie Ashby offered particularly incisive criticisms. (Izzie also indexed the book.) Ffrangcon Lewis proofread the entire manuscript: a herculean feat for someone without any interest in music theory! Gwen Lewis did not read the manuscript, but kept Olly sane.

Research for this book was made possible by a grant from the Deutscher Akademischer Austauschdienst, which enabled JPEH-S to spend an unfeasibly wonderful three months divided between Garmisch-Partenkirchen and Munich. Dominik Šedivý, the director of the Richard Strauss Institute, and Hartmut Schick, of Ludwig Maximilan University, Munich, were extremely generous supporters of the project and hosts at their respective institutions, and they provided the ideal environment in which to engage deeply with Riemann and Strauss's music (where the research began). JPEH-S will never again enjoy such excellent *Kaffee und Kuchen*. He subsequently 'retired' from musicology before finishing this book, and this turned out to be one of his wisest scholarly acts. Olly, who demonstrated early during his doctoral studies to be a more rigorously theorised analyst than his supervisor, offered to take on the responsibility of completing this bit of the *Nachlass*, and he has made transformative improvements to it. Testing and refining its theory through teaching removed many of its rough edges, and his many additional analyses, his restructuring of the whole, and his judicious excerpting of the mass of material (particularly on Waltraute's Plaint) – not to mention his ability to make sense of the often chaotic notes his quasi-posthumous collaborator left behind – have made it far better than it would otherwise have been. JPEH-S therefore wants to single him out for particular thanks, and to tip off reviewers that as a rule of thumb all compliments should be directed to Olly, and all brickbats sent to his undead former supervisor.

Introduction

Among the thorniest problems of music analysis has long been how best to understand music, which ostensibly has a tonal function (and is certainly not, at least at first blush, obviously 'post-tonal') but whose tonal function is attenuated – often extremely so. The general tenor of such music is often as far removed from the reassuring and frequent cadences of Classical and early Romantic music as it could be before the sense that it subscribes to the basic logic of tonality evaporates entirely. Of course, the problem is not merely that examples of late tonality – say, from Wagner to the present – pose problems for analytical comprehension. The rot had set in earlier, and certainly no later than Schubert.

A kind of consensus has emerged that the most profitable way to conceive of the organisation of harmony in music of this kind is to focus on passages where a deeper-level diatonic logic is suspended, held at arm's-length, or even seemingly treated as a curious matter of little concern to the 'real' musical purposes of the piece in question. As Richard Cohn puts it, 'because music of this type uses the harmonic structures and, often, the conventional cadences of diatonic tonality, it lures the attentions of analytical models designed for diatonic music. *Yet it is also notoriously unresponsive to such attentions*'.[1] Marvels unfold from interrogations that are not motivated by such diatonically conceived analytical models. Indeed, work of this kind, which often falls under the broad umbrella of 'neo-Riemannian theory' (NRT), has produced some of the most outstanding new insights into music of the nineteenth and even twentieth centuries. Yet diatonically oriented theories of tonality are more flexible than Cohn perhaps imagines. It strikes us as uncontroversial to assert that diatonic tonality is projected by and through certain patterns of harmonic *function*. Bryan Hyer notes that while such functions were initially associated with diatonic harmonies – namely, Tonic, Subdominant, and Dominant – these *predicates* (i.e. T-ness, S-ness, and D-ness) could be abstracted from their referents over time, becoming *substantiate*.[2] This allows 'us to think of dominant-ness separately, apart from the [...] triad' with which it would be conventionally – diatonically – associated. Crucially, though, the relationship between a dominant-functioning chord and the diatonic-Platonic

DOI: 10.4324/9781003183655-1

dominant that ultimately gave rise to it necessarily persists.³ The former is able to negate the latter, while being unable fully to replace it.

With this subtle enrichment of a basically diatonic theory, it becomes possible to claim that the chromatic music of the later nineteenth century does *not* constitute a Copernican revolution; it can still be conceived of in extended diatonic-functional terms.⁴ Neo-Riemannian theory errs, we suggest, in believing that a tonic–(sub)dominant functional dialectic has either been replaced entirely or has been rendered only infinitesimally significant to the function of certain passages (if not entire pieces). Indeed, on the understanding of late tonal music that we shall argue for in the current book, it is a mistake to allow the possibility that the governing laws of tonality – its functionality – are suspended, even in the extremest moments of chromaticism. Tonality is an ideology of such sophistication and resilience that it would take a stronger force than that exerted by the post-Wagnerians to tear it apart. Were a single passage of a piece to undermine the logic of tonality, then tonality, which is an ideology of *totality*, in which the central idea explains everything, could not be operational in that piece at all; it would be reduced to a surface-level 'topic'.⁵ Indeed, we part company from present-day theorists such as Cohn in suggesting that tonality is not reducible to a single syntax or compositional script – say, a I-IV-V-I bassline, or a descending progression from $\hat{5}$-$\hat{1}$ in the melody – that might be seamlessly substituted for another – say, the physiologically determined pattern of a hand moving smoothly and chromatically across a keyboard, producing one enharmonic paradox after another. Rather, tonality was *the* horizon of musical meaning in the West in the late nineteenth and early twentieth centuries (just as it arguably still is today). In our view, therefore, just as a pre-Copernican conception of the cosmos had accounted for problematic observations by making the geocentric theory more complicated, theories of tonal music should seek ways to become complex enough to account for chromatic musical phenomena without assuming that a new kind of musical logic has become operative.

But there is, of course, a crucial difference between science and music: scientific truths about the cosmos are impersonal; tonality is a fiction of our own creation.⁶ To realise the pre-Copernican error, all one has to do is to look at a scientifically informed representation of our solar system. But even if we were to be shown 'definitive proof' that some passages of late-tonal music might not be tonal at all, the implications of this idea would still be counterintuitive for many listeners.⁷ For such a group of hypothetical but eminently plausible interpreters, the harmonic map for limited spans of music could be imagined – in the words of William Benjamin – as 'a curved space, with a large depression where its tonic is located and smaller ones around the S and D locations, whereby more distant chords gain their psychic charges'.⁸ This perspective synthesises well with the music-theoretical outlook of Hugo Riemann (1849–1919), the original but ultimately distant source of neo-Riemannian theory, who interpreted every possible chord in relation to three possible functions, T, S, and D.

> The map of *neo-Riemannian theory* [by contrast] is flat (or toroidal because of equal temperament), so it is hard to know on what grounds, if any, the objects arrived at through successive transformations acquire a specific charge, whether of tension, distance, or implication.[9]

Undergraduate music students often find the former spatial metaphor intuitive (at least in our experience); it is more difficult to imagine listeners who would accept the latter idea (even after having taken a course in NRT). And in music, unlike in science, that matters a great deal: the function of music theory is not only to provide *new*, hypothetical modes of hearing or to describe how things *might* work – i.e. in the form of abstract, universalizable theories – but also to try to understand the ways in which musical experience is *already* mediated by a historically conditioned (intra-)subjectivity. We will thus invite the reader to consider what is lost if they agree with Cohn's suggestion that late tonal music is 'notoriously unresponsive' to 'diatonically conceived analytical methods'.[10] As an alternative, we advocate for a *return to Riemann*. Through careful consideration of his ideas, and by developing them along a different evolutionary path from that which was taken by NRT, we aim to understand the tonal function of seemingly impossible moments. In so doing, we argue that the expressive, dramatic, and even philosophical and critical-theoretical potentialities of late tonal music can be more precisely and usefully charted and harnessed to both analytical and broader intellectual ends.

Before modelling how such moments might be understood theoretically, however, we need to lay out in more detail the problem that NRT has sought to solve: that is, the problematic question of how we can understand the *function* (or lack thereof) of late tonal music. Given that we have already used this term ten times, it would be timely to provide a working definition. 'Function' is here to be understood in the sense(s) conceived by Riemann, which Bryan Hyer summarises as follows: 'function' does not denote a chord, but rather a chord's 'position as a locus or referent within the aggregate whole [i.e. tonality], something far more abstract than a given major or minor triad'.[11] If tonality, as Riemann conceived it, is a totalising system of musical thought, in which *all* harmonic parameters are caught by the principle of 'function', then any music in which *at least some* harmonic parameters are not caught by the principle of 'function' is not 'tonal'. For NRT, therefore, the suggestion that late tonal music might be thoroughgoingly (as opposed to sporadically) functional is logically invalid.

Over the course of the next five chapters, we dispute this syllogism. After briefly sketching, defending, and adapting Riemann's theories (including *Funktionstheorie*) in Chapter 1, Chapter 2 lays out the book's essential argument: namely, that some chromatic events can be understood as 'determinate

4 *Introduction*

negations' of tonality. To adapt the words of Andrew Bowie, late tonal music is 'limited to the refusal to follow the direction given by [traditional, diatonic tonality], while yet depending on it as what it has to leave behind to make any sense at all'.[12] In other words, marked chromatic events challenge traditional harmonic-functional frameworks without creating new patterns that suggest the existence of a fully worked-out, *competing* framework. Riemann's function theory provides a wonderfully clear means of representing this negative-dialectical relationship. ('Negative' because it does not give rise to a new framework, but forces us inventively to exhaust the existing one.) To make our point, we leap into one of the most complex passages of chromatic music in Wagner's opera, *Götterdämmerung*: namely, Waltraute's Plaint. In response to this scene's idiosyncrasies, we develop a theory of functional 'moons', adapting Richard Cohn's original conception of hexatonic 'space' to our Riemannian functional paradigm. We call the resultant model *lunar tonality*, and we discuss individual chords and their composite trajectories in terms of 'light-side' and 'dark-side' functions.

Chapter 3 demonstrates how Wagner's rotations round the far-flung peripheries of the functional moons hypothesised in Chapter 2 are paralleled by more strongly centred but still notably chromatic passages in more generally diatonic music: extracts from Beethoven's Op. 10, No. 1 and Brahms's Double Concerto for Violin and Cello, Op. 102 are adduced in support of this claim. In relation to the latter piece, in particular, the authors critique NRT's tendency to abstract short, chromatic excerpts from their broader harmonic and formal contexts, and thus to brush over their dialectical interaction with more conventional tonal materials.

Moving beyond triads, Chapter 4 considers Riemann's attitude to seventh chords and outlines common critiques of his position, especially from the NRT perspective: this includes his claims that diminished and augmented triads are not a separate 'species' of chord, and that sevenths are *necessarily* extensions of triads, as opposed to being special musical objects with their own properties. The representation of a total network of smooth voice-leading connection in a post-*Tristan* world, offered by Cohn as a counter to these claims, is invaluable. But we attempt to reinject functional energy into his representation of tetrachordal pitch space by re-conceptualising its harmonic nodes as a field of 'submoons' that orbit the triadic functional moons hypothesised in Chapter 2. This allows us to explain the functional significations of chords that move 'smoothly' (as in Chopin's Op. 28, No. 4) and those which are highly disjunct but still acutely chromatic (the 'Hagen Chords' motif as it appears in Act 1, Scene 3 of *Götterdämmerung*), while avoiding some of the pitfalls of a purely Riemannian approach: e.g. the excessive number of possible functional labels that can result if a seventh is understood as being derived from one of many possible triadic formations.

In Chapter 5, we consider another common criticism of Riemannian analysis: namely, its tendency to focus on functional description *in the moment*.

If tonality is a totalising system that relates part to whole, then Riemann's prospective (as opposed to retrospective) listening bias is surely a handicap; one cannot get beyond rich descriptions of atomistic moments. In response to this criticism, we develop a hybrid notation, drawing on Schenkerian and Riemannian principles. To map the large-scale contrapuntal structures that are unfolded in a near one-hundred-bar excerpt from Wagner's *Götterdämmerung*, we draw on a proto-Schenkerian notation; but, because of the music's pervasive chromaticism, *Stufen* (scale-steps) are replaced by *functions*. An additional set of notational symbols are developed in order to show how a 'pure' function can be prolonged by chords that we describe (after Riemann) as 'enriched' or (following a more Wagnerian logic) 'corrupted'. (These terms map onto the dark-side functions theorised in earlier chapters.) On our journey towards the formulation of this system, we critique and adapt famous Schenkerian analyses of Wagnerian opera by Patrick McCreless and Warren Darcy.

In a nutshell: the book searches for function in chromatic music, beginning with foreground 'pan-triadic' progressions and moving on to those that involve sevenths, before concluding with the consideration of much broader spans of music from a more contrapuntal perspective. We start from Riemannian principles, but we conclude by stretching those principles to their elastic limit. In so doing, we attempt to demonstrate the totalising logic of tonality.

Notes

1 Richard Cohn, 'Introduction to Neo-Riemannian Theory: A Survey and a Historical Perspective', *Journal of Music Theory* 42, no. 2 (1998): 167–80, 168, our emphasis.
2 Bryan Hyer, 'What Is a Function?', *The Oxford Handbook to Neo-Riemannian Music Theories*, eds. Edward Gollin and Alexander Rehding (Oxford: Oxford University Press, 2011), 92–139, 98.
3 Ibid., 101.
4 We have in mind Immanuel Kant's comparison of the paradigm shift in his thought to that of Copernicus's replacement of the geocentric with his heliocentric model of the solar system: see Imannuel Kant, *Critique of Pure Reason*, ed. Paul Guyer and Allen W. Wood (Cambridge: Cambridge University Press, 1998), 113. Our analogous claim is this: that for late tonal music to effect a Copernican revolution, it would have to reorientate musical orbits around something other than the tonic-dominant dialectic, but that it does not.
5 See Thomas Johnson, 'Tonality as Topic: Opening a World of Analysis for Early Twentieth-Century Modernist Music', *Music Theory Online* 23, no. 4 (2017). https://mtosmt.org/issues/mto.17.23.4/mto.17.23.4.johnson.html.
6 Richard Cohn, 'Peter, the Wolf, and the Hexatonic Uncanny', in *Tonality 1900–1950: Concept and Practice*, eds. Felix Wörner, Ullrich Scheideler, and Philip Rupprecht (Stuttgart: Franz Steiner Verlag, 2012), 47–62, particularly 47–8.
7 For the example of such 'proof', see Cohn's discussion of Agmon's principle in 'Hexatonic Uncanny', 49.
8 William Benjamin, 'Review: *The Oxford Handbook to Neo-Riemannian Music Theories*', *Journal of Music Theory* 58, no. 1 (2014): 237.

6 *Introduction*

  9 Ibid., our emphasis.
10 Cohn took tonality down off the shelf in some of his later publications, particularly Chapter 8 of *Audacious Euphony: Chromaticism and the Triad's Second Nature* (Oxford: Oxford University Press, 2012); but his concept of code switching (see his Chapter 9), while allowing for the integration of tonal and 'post-tonal' syntaxes, still relies on their fundamental separability: tonality is based on diatonic scale-degree theory, whereas chromatic logic is founded on smooth voice leading. This argument is critiqued in Chapters 2 and 4 of the current book.
11 Hyer, 'What Is a Function?', 98.
12 Andrew Bowie, *Adorno: A Very Short Introduction* (Oxford: Oxford University Press, 2022), 98.

Bibliography

Benjamin, William. 'Review: *The Oxford Handbook to Neo-Riemannian Music Theories*', *Journal of Music Theory* 58, no. 1 (2014): 235–56.

Bowie, Andrew. *Adorno: A Very Short Introduction*. Oxford: Oxford University Press, 2022.

Cohn, Richard. 'Introduction to Neo-Riemannian Theory: A Survey and a Historical Perspective', *Journal of Music Theory* 42, no. 2 (1998): 167–80.

———. *Audacious Euphony: Chromaticism and the Triad's Second Nature*. Oxford: Oxford University Press, 2012.

———. 'Peter, the Wolf, and the Hexatonic Uncanny', in *Tonality 1900–1950: Concept and Practice*, edited by Felix Wörner, Ullrich Scheideler, and Philip Rupprecht, 47–62. Stuttgart: Franz Steiner Verlag, 2012.

Hyer, Bryan. 'What Is a Function?' in *The Oxford Handbook to Neo-Riemannian Music Theories*, edited by Edward Gollin, and Alexander Rehding, 92–139. Oxford: Oxford University Press, 2011.

Johnson, Thomas. 'Tonality as Topic: Opening a World of Analysis for Early Twentieth-century Modernist Music', *Music Theory Online* 23, no. 4 (2017). https://mtosmt.org/issues/mto.17.23.4/mto.17.23.4.johnson.html.

Kant, Immanuel. *Critique of Pure Reason*, edited by Paul Guyer, and Allen W. Wood. Cambridge: Cambridge University Press, 1998.

1 Riemannian Theory and the Problem of Chromatic Function

A Brief Overview of Riemann's Music-Theoretical Project

This book is not a history. Comprehensive accounts of Riemann's career and of the development of his various theories are already available; many of them will be cited in the coming pages. We merely sketch his ideas here in order to provide a context for our own Riemann-inspired theorising later in the book. As Alexander Rehding argues in *Hugo Riemann and the Birth of Modern Musical Thought*, Riemann's music-theoretical corpus represents a fraught and often contradictory balancing act. On the one hand, aspects of his work (i.e. harmonic dualism and the *Schritt/Wechsel* system, defined below) displayed a positivistic commitment to quantifying, mapping, and explaining the drastically expanded harmonic resources of the 'modern, free tonality' of his own epoch.[1] On the other hand, some of this theoretical ideas (i.e. *Funktionstheorie*, also defined below) are much more impressionistic; they were developed in order to mitigate the 'musico-moral' fallout that resulted from the aforementioned expansion of harmonic resources. Riemann seems to have believed that if any consonant chord was permitted to follow any other – as some of Riemann's contemporaries claimed was possible[2] – then 'social-democratic' chaos would result. The implication is that tonal and social hierarchies are metalogically related.[3] By relating all chromatic chords to only three diatonic functions – T, S, and D – he sought to shore up musical logic, reifying the harmonic language of First Viennese Classicism as a universal truth. (The radical claim of Riemann's contemporaries was not thereby invalidated, however – it was justified in relation to a 'Classicising' metric.)

Harmonic Dualism

The positivistic strand of Riemann's music-theoretical thought relied on the acoustical 'justifications' for which he is now infamous: his belief in so-called *harmonic dualism*. For Riemann, as for many other nineteenth-century thinkers, the major triad was 'given in nature': its intervallic structure replicated the first five partials of the harmonic series (the fundamental frequency of which is the first partial). His logic runs as follows: if one judges harmonic proximity on the basis of whether the distribution of fundamental bass tones in a series of chords replicates the ordering of the overtone series, then the triads built on the 2nd and

DOI: 10.4324/9781003183655-2

8 Riemannian Theory and the Problem of Chromatic Function

4th overtones – the perfect fifth and the major third – will be the most stable in relation to a given tonic: e.g. G major and E major in the key of C major.

Minor chords, he further claims, should not be understood as artificial perversions of the major triad 'given in nature'; we can derive them, quite simply, by inverting the 'Chord of Nature' back around its fundamental, e.g. {C}: <C,E,G> becomes <C,A♭,F>, $I_{C/C}$.[4] (For this reason, major chords are generated 'upwards' from their prime – e.g. <C,E,G> – and minor chords are generated 'downwards' from their prime – e.g. <C,A♭,F>; the root of both chords is {C}).[5] This *undertone series* is also given in nature; but it is harder to perceive; hence, Riemann's being the first to discover it.[6]

If one accepts that mapping the intervallic structure of this Nature-given triad onto its 2nd and 4th *over*tones produces those chords most closely related to a given tonic, then one can hypothesise that the same should be true of those chords built on the 2nd and 4th notes of the *under*tone series, too. In C major, for example, this means that E major (replicating the 4th 'overtone') and A♭ major (replicating the 4th 'undertone') are the closest harmonies to the tonic after G major (the 2nd overtone, i.e. the dominant) and F minor (the 2nd undertone, i.e. the undertonal dominant). Similarly, B major and E♭ major are most proximate to 'Chord V' (G major) after D major (the over-fifth, or secondary dominant) and C major (the under-fifth, or subdominant of the dominant). Bringing this logic full circle, A major and D♭ major are nearest 'Chord IV' (F major) after C major (the over-fifth, or dominant of the subdominant) and B♭ major (the under-fifth, or subdominant of the subdominant). When dealing with relations of this kind, Riemann argues that 'figuring in the sense of one scale is not possible'.[7] Diatonicism, the bedrock of Weberian Roman-Numeral analysis, is obviated.[8] The *Tonnetz* [tone grid], by contrast, which Riemann first began to use in his 1874 *Über das Musikalische Hören*, accommodates this expanded list of free-tonal options with ease (see Figure 1.1).[9] The relative proximity of any two letter names supposedly denotes

his	fisis	cisis	gisis	disis	aisis	aisis	hisis	f♯♯♯♯
gis	dis	ais	eis	his	fisis	cisis	gisis	disis
e	h	fis	cis	gis	dis	ais	eis	his
c	g	d	a	e	h	fis	cis	gis
as	es	b	f	c	g	d	a	e
fes	ces	ges	des	as	es	b	f	c
deses	asas	eses	heses	fes	ces	ges	des	as
♭♭♭h	feses	ceses	geses	deses	asas	eses	heses	fes

Figure 1.1 An early *Tonnetz* from Riemann's *Allgemeine Musiklehre* (1888), 69, reproduced in Kopp, *Chromatic Transformations*, 77 (Plate 4.1). Reproduced by permission of Cambridge University Press.

the relative closeness of their tonal relationship. But, as Alexander Rehding has noted, 'in its infinite dimensions, allowing virtually any kind of harmonic relation, the "grid" does not in fact explain anything': the notion of a meaningful hierarchy becomes untenable.[10]

The *Schritt/Wechsel* System

Riemann's *Schritt/Wechsel* [step/change] system – first outlined in 1880 in the *Skizze einer neuen Methode der Harmonielehre*, but utilised and developed throughout the rest of his life – attempted to circumscribe these possibilities in a more consistent way. Riemann used the first term (*Schritt*) to describe how many 'steps' the root of one chord is from another; the latter term (*Wechsel*) determines whether there is a 'change of mode'. An exhaustive, unwieldy system of naming resulted (e.g. a *Kleinterzwechsel* [a minor-third root progression with a mode change] takes C major to D minor: NB: the fifth of the latter chord, {A}, functions as its undertonal root); but chordal relationships could still not be explained or predicted, merely described. While it is exactly this neutral means of labelling relationships that so appealed to later neo-Riemannian theorists, Riemann himself found it disquieting.[11] As in political life, he thought, a lack of hierarchy in music – the absence of a pre-given structure in which the individual can find their meaning – threatened one's sense of orientation.

In a further attempt to shore up musical logic, Riemann began to label all chromatic chords as modifications of the 'primary' functions – T, S, and D – within the diatonic scale; he generated a new music-theoretical language in the process, which he called *Funktionstheorie*.[12] Multiple possibilities are reduced to few; the traversal of many different harmonic paths might ultimately be shown to trace the same cadential journey.

Funktionstheorie

In this book, we shall make extensive use of Riemann's *Funktionstheorie* terminology. Some of it will need to be defended against common criticisms and/or rehabilitated through the introduction of additional parameters to narrow down the number of possible functions (especially in richly chromatic music); other aspects will require clarification and, in some cases, the modification of familiar neo-Riemannian terms. Let us begin, more simply, with the latter task.

Although, of course, and by definition, the basic P, L, and R transformations of NRT have their origin in Riemann's work, his use, and the use we shall advance here, is different in one very important respect: each of these transformations links chords that, irrespective of the transformational link between them, have a function within a certain precisely defined tonality. This function serves as the 'truth' of their harmonic unfolding.[13] Tonality itself is governed by three functions, with Tonic (T), Subdominant (S), and Dominant (D) accounting, somehow or other, for the function of every conceivable tonal chord. Put more boldly, and technically: all possible chords can be related, through the (semi)tonal adjustment of their voices, to these three functions. A practical example will help to make this last point clear.

Imagine an F-minor tonality: {F,A♭,C} = °T; {B♭,D♭,F} = °S; {C,E♭,G} = °D (NB: the degree symbol to the lefthand-side of the function symbol indicates that the chord in question is minor; a plus to the righthand-side of a function symbol [e.g. T$^+$], or no symbol at all [e.g. T], by contrast, would indicate that it was major. For a glossary of Riemannian notations, see p. 87.)

Now, imagine the secondary triads in F-minor: {G,B♭,D}; {A♭,C,E♭}; {D♭,F,A♭}, {E♭,G,B♭}.

Riemann would interpret these chords as *blends* of two primary functions: i.e. of T and S, or T and D, or S and D. Chord III, {A♭,C,E♭}, for example, shares two notes with °T and two with °D. Here are the voice leadings that connect A♭ to these two functions:

{F,A♭,C}→{E♭,A♭,C}: in this case, °T is modified; its root descends by a whole tone. (NB: we underline those notes that *will be* and *have been* modified.)

{C,E♭,G}→{C,E♭,A♭}: in this case, °D is modified; its fifth ascends by a semitone.

How can one represent these changes in functional notation? First, we must consider all the functional modifications possible in the Riemannian harmonic universe:

Leading-tone transformation: The root of a major triad *descends* a semitone; the fifth of a minor triad *ascends* a semitone (e.g. {C,E,G}→{B,E,G}; {C,E♭,G}→{C,E♭,A♭}). Each possibility is indicated by an overlaid less- or more-than sign, depending on whether the moving voice falls (<) or rises (>) to the leading tone: e.g. E minor would be ⋦, whereas A♭ major would be °⋧.[14] (N.B.: Cohn, a neo-Riemannian theorist, uses the transformational label L to describe these relationships.)

Parallel transformation: The fifth of a major triad ascends a whole tone; the root of a minor triad descends a whole tone (e.g. {C,E,G}→{C,E,A}; {C,E♭,G}→{B♭,E♭,G}. Major is exchanged for relative minor; minor for relative major. A parallel transformation is indicated by a p suffix: e.g. °A would be C$^+$p, and E♭$^+$ would °Cp. (N.B.: Cohn would use the label R to describe these transformations: 'relative' in English has the same meaning as 'parallel' in German.)

Variant transformation: This alters the mode of a chord *after* another transformation (either leading-tone or parallel) has already been performed: e.g. the °A chord of the previous example becomes A$^+$; the E♭$^+$ of the previous example will become °E♭. A subscript, italicised v indicates that a variant transformation has taken place: e.g. C$^+$p$_v$ and °Cp$_v$. (NB: Cohn would refer to these as Parallel, or P, transformations.[15])

We are now in a position to return to the possible functional designations for A♭$^+$, namely:

{F,A♭,C}→{A♭,C,E♭} = °Tp
{C,E♭,G→A♭} = °𝔇

Now, imagine that A♭⁺ becomes °A♭. This would result in a °Tp_v or °𝔇_v function. Indeed, if °A♭ were to appear as part of a progression from °F to °C, then one could even argue that it was serving as some kind of chromatic mediator: i.e. it is *on its the way* to the dominant, meaning that it is *no longer* T, but it is *not yet* D.[16] Riemann designates this possibility with an italicised *3*. And, since the resulting dominant has been prepared by a 'scale-denying' third chord, he suggests, uniquely, notating 'D' as *5*.[17] Hence, even so basic a function as the dominant can have a different notation. (Two other notations that we sometimes have recourse to use in this book are 𝕊 and 𝔻 : i.e. the subdominant of the subdominant, or dominant of the dominant.)

It is important to clarify here that °A♭ – designated variously as 'Tp_v', '°𝔇_v', or '*3*' – is not *literally* a tonic, dominant, or mediating chord. The labels in question indicate merely that it *might* work to project such functions (the 'function' in question being the *general* 'truth' lying behind a *particular* chord's intervallic and acoustic qualities).[18] This gives Riemann's functional theory a fundamentally different view of the 'meaning' of tonality from that familiarly adopted in NRT, in which there is only one relation between, for example, the chords C⁺ and °E: i.e. that of the *Leittonwechsel* function.

What if the tonal implication of a given passage shifts: e.g. T functions as a pivot chord in the toncisation of S? In Riemann's words: ' [intermediate] *cadences to ... harmonies hitherto characterised according to their position in the key* [e.g. S, D, 𝔇 , etc.]... *are to be considered as tonics, without, however, their* [original] *tonal functions being altered*'.[19] For example, if a °G-C⁺-F⁺ progression were to be interpolated into a C-major tonality, then its final chord might be understood both as a local tonic and as, more generally, S. To convey this double-function, one can use the following notation: i.e. (Sp-D)S. The brackets indicate that °G and C⁺ function as Sp and D *of* F⁺; F⁺ itself, however, functions as S in C⁺. Such parenthetical functions might also relate to the chord *before* a parenthesis. If so, this is indicated by an arrow: e.g. S→(D): the latter chord is a back-relating dominant to the preceding S. Where a chord functions as a pivot between two keys (e.g. C⁺ as T of C⁺ and S of G⁺) its dual function is indicated by an equals sign: e.g. T(=S)D. (This progression might also be notated as T=S-T: the functions after the equals sign are both written in the new key.)

Finally, Riemann does not admit into his functional system a third or fourth species of chord: i.e. diminished and augmented triads, or dissonant sevenths. Every sonority, no matter how altered or extended, is to be interpreted in relation to an embedded or implied consonant triad. Simple functions such as D⁷ need no clarification, but Riemann's other labels are less intuitive. An augmented triad built on the tonic degree, for example, might be notated as $T^{5<}$. The superscript less-than symbol indicates the semitonal raising of the chordal fifth; a superscript more-than symbol, by contrast, would indicate a semitonal lowering, as in the case of a diminished triad: e.g. a {E,G,B♭} chord in °E would be $T^{5>}$. But the functional meaning of a diminished triad is particularly dependent on tonal context. In F major, for example, {E,G,B♭} might be understood either as a dominant seventh without a root (i.e. Ð⁷: the excision is marked by a slash), or as a subdominant under-seventh without its prime, {D}, hence °S̶p̶^{VII}.[20] (If the {D} had been present in the latter chord, it would have been labelled °Sp^{VII}: Riemann's notation for what contemporary music theory would call a half-diminished seventh.) The sheer number of possible functional interpretations that Riemann's triadic mode of labelling sevenths gives rise to makes some theorists doubt the efficacy of his system. These critiques are outlined in Chapter 4.

Neo-Riemannian Analysis and Riemann's Tonal Functions[21]

Considering Riemann's (hypothetical) commitment to mapping the functional relations not only of common-practice tonality but also of what he called 'free tonality'[22] – i.e. the chromatic music of the nineteenth and early twentieth centuries – it is remarkable that, on the whole, neo-Riemannian theory has devoted relatively little attention to this part of Riemann's system.[23] For there to be tonality on Riemann's understanding, very little is required. If a piece of music contains triads, or chords that can be heard as combinations of triads, then there is tonality. (One can almost hear Tonality saying: 'For where two or three triads are gathered together in my name, there I am in the midst of them' [Matthew 18:20]). And if there is tonality, then the three basic functions of Tonic, Subdominant, and Dominant are invoked, and every possible configuration will be legible with respect to one of those functions, as a parallel, leading-tone change, or variant (or some compound of these). There can exist nothing in tonal music that is not captured by one of the three functions; everything is 'totalised' by them. Freedom from these functions, which hold tonality in place, is illusory. Tonality is virtually omnipotent. This might be, and perhaps should be, an unnerving realisation, but it is also one that argues strongly for a genuinely Riemannian, not a neo-Riemannian, approach to the analysis of late-tonal music, because as well as enabling an insight into what is most remarkable about individual pieces of music, it holds out the possibility of understanding the functions of that power vividly and systematically.

And yet the process by which all chords that are *not* the diatonic Tonic, Subdominant, or Dominant are understood to submit their individuality to the overall function of the triumvirs might sometimes imply the parallel existence of a nonfunctional, and ultimately relativistic, tonal space. This is particularly the case when a chromatic chord might actually be related to a number of different diatonic functions, in which case the apparent arbitrariness of applying functional labels is taken as a death knell for the functional system as a whole. We will further explore this common criticism below, considering how our Riemannian commitment might be adapted in response to it through the theorisation of two principal chord-labelling constraints.

Constraint No. 1: Harmony, Functional Identity, and Octatonic Area

Alexander Rehding cites the harmonic excursions of Beethoven's Op. 26/iii – a piece that Riemann himself analysed – as marking a point of impasse for Riemann's system of *Tonalität*. This is because a functional analysis of its opening harmonic waystations appears to collapse under the weight of its own contradictions (see Figure 1.2):

> If we were to continue our path along the exact transposition, with which the music continues, without positing a modulation, we would soon end up with impossible functions, that is, with multiple *Scheinkonsonanzen* [illusory consonances]... It is not surprising that Riemann was reluctant to pursue this analysis in any greater detail. The resulting analysis would bring the theory of function closer to the modern idea of transformations and further away from Riemann's long-held ideas of *Tonalität*.[24]

The modern idea of transformation, as applied to this progression, consists of the following premises: (1) Chords connect to one another through a limited number of (generally smooth) voice-leading operations, applied singly or in combination; (2) The chords 'as objects' are secondary to the relations that inhere between them; (3) These operations do not necessarily invoke a tonal context; they occur at the level of chord rather than key. Some of these ideas – namely, (1) and (2) – are implicit in Rehding's hypothetical Riemannian

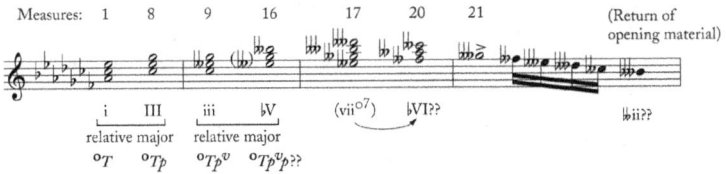

Figure 1.2 Alexander Rehding's Riemannian analysis of Beethoven's Piano Sonata in A♭ major, Op. 26, bb. 1–21 (Example 4(b), 117 in the original). Reproduced by permission of University of California Press.

labels, shown above; but (3) is inimical to them – the labels suggest that the progression 'prolongs' a single function (Tonic, in this case).

A sceptic may rightly question how A♭ minor and D major can be understood to have the same function; but does reducing this passage to a string of transformations, divorced from an underlying object that is 'transformed', get us to the heart of what makes this progression what it is? If chords float monadically in a symmetrically neutral voice-leading space, then surely any chord within it would become as apposite as any other (i.e. they would all have the same effect)? Alternatively, one might say that P-R-P-R cycles have an overall quality *as a cycle*; but surely each chord in the chain signifies differently, as we move farther away from (or come back towards) a putative tonic?

Kenneth Smith's rigorously theorised concept of harmonic function provides an excellent means of arguing for the hypothetical Riemannian labelling that Rehding takes to be improbable.[25] To understand how chords may be functionally equivalent, he considers it essential first to consider the most common chord substitutions in common-practice music and in jazz. If one wants the subdominant of C major to have a darker tinge, one substitutes ii for IV (D minor for F major). If one wants IV$^6_5$ to lead with greater melodic intensity to V, then one flattens the 'bass' and sharpens the 'soprano' to create an augmented sixth, ♭VI^7 (F major becomes A♭^{7}). If one articulates IV as a seventh chord (as one might in a Blues progression), then its constituent tritone can be reharmonised as part of a VII$^{\flat 7}_{\sharp 3}$ chord, *à la* tritone substitution (F^7 becomes B^7). These minor-3rd related chords (D, A♭, and B) appear equally capable of substituting for F, albeit in quite different situations. Is there a quality that these chords share, irrespective of the voice-leading context or genre in which they appear, that vouchsafes their functional *sameness*?

It is at this point that Smith shifts from the empirical to the abstract. Discharge from one function to another (T, S, or D), he argues, is facilitated most strongly by leading-tone resolution: ♯$\hat{7}$-$\hat{8}$; ♭$\hat{6}$-$\hat{5}$. *Minor-third-related chords*, such as those that Beethoven cycles through in Op. 26/iii, *do not contain one another's leading tones*; ergo, they prolong the same function. If one were to agglomerate all of the pitch classes in these various chords, then an octatonic scale would be the result. There are three octatonic scales and there are three tonal functions; they map onto one another isomorphically.[26]

Smith's theory of leading-tone discharge (and its obverse: octatonic stasis) allows us to understand how seemingly distantly related chords might still manifest the same function.[27] Rehding's implicit claim that °Tp$_v$p is not a possible label for D major – 'Surely the basic function *must* have changed after so many modifications?' – is no longer self-evidently true. While the accumulation of functional modifiers *might* lead to a logically untenable functional designation, if those chords all belong to the same octatonic group, then there are definite grounds for thinking of them as being *potentially* equivalent, while also qualitatively distinct: something that Riemannian labels, which emphasise the voice-leading proximity of an often chromatic chord to an original, diatonic function, capture nicely.

Constraint No. 2: Counterpoint, Functional Identity, and Hexatonic 8-7/5-6 Suspensions

Not all chords are 'chords'; some are products of counterpoint. We argue that *contrapuntal* chords develop a function associated with a *harmonic* chord that has already been heard, rather than suggesting a new one of their own. Take the hypothetical four-part progression in Example 1.1.[28] A leading-tone transformation takes C⁺ to °E in bar 1. On Smith's model, this would imply a change of function, from T to D. But contrapuntal context makes it plain that the broader motion is from C⁺ (T) to °A (Tp); the B in the melody is arguably used merely to prevent the parallel octaves that would otherwise arise between the first and third tonic-functioning chords (8–5–8). (°A itself represents a 5–6 elaboration of the Tonic.) The G♯ inflection does not affect this; it merely increases the melodic pull towards the Tonic's *parallel*.

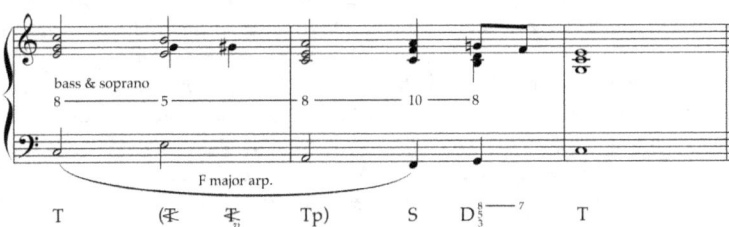

Example 1.1 Hypothetical four-part progression demonstrating Riemannian voice-leading principles.

In *Harmony Simplified*, Riemann offers the following perceptive statement: 'The introduction of parallel clangs … signifies a very considerable *enrichment* of the means of cadential formation and *a more detailed subdivision of them*'.[29] He schematises this idea as follows:

Tp enters between T and S
Sp '' '' S '' D
Dp '' '' D '' T

The concepts of enrichment and subdivision here suggest that alterations (i.e. contrapuntal chords) will modify a function that has already been heard, while also bridging towards a new function that will often be presented in its most lucid, diatonic form.[30] But could we not take Riemann's logic to an extreme: what stops F⁺ from being heard as Ḏp, instead of S, for example, given that it serves to break the octaves between Tp and D? Again, contrapuntal context provides a ready answer. The bass clearly arpeggiates an F-major chord between bars 1^1–2^3. Because the A is *interior* to the melodic motion, <C, A, F>, it does not control the function of the final chord, which relates back to the first chord of the progression: i.e. we understand F⁺ as S of T, rather than as Ḏp of Tp.

While 'secondary triads [e.g. °E in C major] are such simultaneous representatives of two of the three primary chords', as William C. Mickelson puts it, it is often the case that 'one is comprehended as the main content (consonance), the other as a foreign addition (dissonance)'.[31] In this case, °E is heard as an *enrichment* of the foregoing C⁺. So, while °E can be identified with dominant function because it contains 7̂/C (as Smith would argue), this is a 'foreign addition' to the 'main content'. Rather than representing a full dominant chord, L instead *inflects* the Tonic towards the Dominant. In other words, it is a question of *attitude* (the *modification* of a basic functional symbol) as opposed to *ontology* (the *change* of basic functional symbol). It is this conception of chordal function – in which a 'Platonic' clang might be identified with, and thus critiqued by, a shadowy simulacrum – that makes Riemannian analysis such a powerful analytical tool.[32]

In summary, most progressions will proceed from a point of stability to a point of 'enrichment' (or corruption, depending on one's perspective) as a means of extending a given functional progression in time. One can distinguish between what is enriched and what is enriching by examining the given voice-leading situation in which chords are embedded. One might retort that this rationale works well for the basically diatonic and cadential progression modelled in Example 1.1, but that it would become strained when applied to something so tonally wayward as Wagner. This points to a tension right at the heart of Riemann's theory: the (often uneasy) relationship between 'speculative theory and practical instruction in four-part writing'.[33] But perhaps these things are not so far away from one another as is often supposed. Adorno wrote in his *Versuch*:

> [Wagner's] mature works, even where the orchestration is at its richest, are always based on an almost academic adherence to the four-voice harmonic texture. ... It might often appear as if by the textbook setting of chords that break all the rules the harmonic revolutionary were anxious to placate the teachers he had escaped.[34]

While this is intended as a criticism, it is possible to think about this judgement more positively: if counterpoint gives one the means to enrich a given function, then Wagner's chromatic magic might be seen as a further intensification of this enrichment. Take the following (idealised) reduction, based on a progression from Waltraute's Plaint (see Example 1.2).

Riemannian Theory and the Problem of Chromatic Function 17

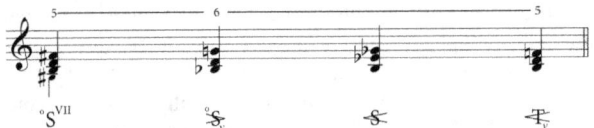

Example 1.2 Idealised reduction of a progression from Waltraute's Plaint, *Götterdämmerung*, Act 1, Scene 3, bb. 1238–40.

If we eliminate the first chord's G♯ – a characteristic, 'undertonal' dissonance – then the progression we're left with is °B, °G, °E♭, B♭⁺. In part-writing terms, we can understand the outer voices of the °G and °E♭ triads as presenting various flavours of sixth, which break the fifths between °B and B♭⁺. (As in the earlier example, 'enriching' harmonies are used to prevent unwanted parallels.) We move from our pure subdominant (with under-seventh) through remote Subdominant functions before alighting on a weak tonic. Metrically, rhetorically, and harmonically, this is a clear plagal cadence; but the relation of this 'Tonic-functioning' chord to the actual Tonic, °F♯ is more obscure: something that the label 𝔗ᵥ captures nicely. ('Home came he at last', says Waltraute of Wotan; but on his return to Valhalla, the latter was no longer the same…) Smith's octatonic theory, by contrast, would fix this progression's meaning as S→D→T←D, with the plagal resolution emphasising *the dominant*. For us, the original Riemannian conception captures better the feeling of moving progressively from a pure to an enriched (Subdominant) function via implicitly contrapuntal chords, as well as the provisionality of the final chord, which is rhetorically and metrically 'Tonic' while containing one subdominant tone ($♭\hat{6}$) and one dominant ($\hat{7}$).

Significantly, the examples of functional enrichment detailed here work according to a decidedly hexatonic logic: °B, °G, and °E♭ are all major-third-related. As already discussed, Smith generalises that all minor-third-related root motions *prolong* function. Concomitantly, major-third-related motions *rotate* function (i.e. the relevant chords are drawn from different underlying octatonic scales). This is a hypothesis that we often assent to; but it is important to acknowledge that there are some voice-leading contexts in which hexatonic-style progressions might function prolongationally too, especially if they involve (chromaticised) $\hat{5}$-$\hat{6}$/$\hat{8}$-$\hat{7}$ progressions.

Tritone Resolution and Tonicisation

A pressing question must be answered at this juncture: how does cadential voice leading factor into Riemann's system? Surely the $\hat{4}$-$\hat{3}$/$\hat{7}$-$\hat{1}$ tritone resolution, native to the diatonic scale, is largely responsible for tonicisation? (One can think of such resolutions as 'quilting points' that draw all surrounding chords into a meaningful constellation.) If such tonicisation does not occur – as it cannot in symmetrical scales such as the hexatonic and octatonic – then the strength of any putative tonality is surely doubtful?

We concur that tritone resolutions can inspire a sense of tonality; but we argue that they are not essential to tonality's manifestation. First, tritone resolutions can also occur in post-tonal contexts: e.g., a French Sixth {C#,G,B,F} resolving to a cluster chord {C,C#,D,D#,E} might technically manifest a contrapuntal resolution, {B,F}→{C,E}, while still producing an obvious increase in harmonic dissonance. (Cohn would point out the unviability of a tonal interpretation here because of the impossibility of non-arbitrarily ascribing diatonic scale degrees to a [012345] set class.[35]) Second, tonality can exist *without* tritones: Schenker's *Ursatz* is supposed to compose-out *the* perfect tonal structure; and yet tritones manifest merely as inner-voice filler within it.

To put the case plainly: tonality is often strengthened by the presence of resolving (or deliberately frustrated) tritones. Their absence, however, does not make something 'non-tonal'; the functional differences that result from tritone absence/presence are spectral rather than absolute. Furthermore, we take Kopp's lead in suggesting that the ways in which chromatic mediants voice lead to their 'tonics' often demonstrate important kinships with standard D-T and S-T relations: namely, the retention of a common tone between the two chords; the traversal of a consonant interval between the chords' bass notes; and a semitonal resolution from one to the other, which effects a leading-tone-like discharge.[36] This accounts, along with the voice-leading constraints theorised above, for the functional significations of chromatic triadic progressions.

Stretching the Relation between 'Enriching' and 'Enriched' Chords

A possible criticism of Riemann's ideas about so-called enriching harmonies might be that there are frequently circumstances in which chromatic chords *do not* enrich an already heard diatonic function. Take the S^1 theme of Fanny Hensel's Piano Trio, Op. 11 (1846–7), for example (see Example 1.3). The 'consequent phrase' of its allusively periodic structure progresses thus: F, F^7, B♭^{6}, E^7, A. Imagined as a string of Riemannian functions, this would yield T, T^7, S^6, ᖰ$_v^7$, 𝔗$_v$. The two concluding functions of the chain do not enrich preceding diatonic chords; they stand on their own as independent entities. The theme's aforementioned periodic quality, however, ensures that this phrase is heard as the parallel of the earlier 'antecedent phrase'. In other words, the harmonies of the 'consequent' are associated with those of the foregoing 'antecedent' (i.e. T, T^6_4, °S^6, D^7); that which is 'enriching' still relates to an 'enriched', albeit that the latter stands at a temporal remove. Of course, as the nineteenth century wore on, it became increasingly likely that 'enriching chords' would behave like *Scheinkonsonanzen* [feigning consonances]: i.e. they are conceptually elided with, but materially replace, a fundamental, diatonic function. (For this reason, they are 'dissonant', even if they *sound* like a consonant triad.) And yet, this passage demonstrates – albeit on a small scale – how the link between 'enriching' and 'enriched' chords might have first been stretched.

Riemannian Theory and the Problem of Chromatic Function 19

Example 1.3 Hensel, Piano Trio, Op. 11, i, Allegro molto vivace, bb. 58–66.

After a quasi-transitional passage, S² tonicises D♭ (see Example 1.4). One might view the resulting middle-ground major-third complex (F, A, D♭) as being derived from a hexatonic scale: i.e. a symmetrical, non-hierarchical, and thus afunctional pitch collection. Its phrasal grammar, however, makes it unlikely that a listener would hear it as such. S² is also periodically organised: a compound antecedent closes with a i:IAC; the consequent finishes deceptively, (S-D)°𝄇. Scholars such as Richard Cohn might argue that D♭'s tonicity is rhetorical rather than structural: it results from the consequent's metric and dynamic shape, rather than from its relationship to F⁺.[37] This much is true – but the easy retort is that pitch cannot be experienced separately from these other parameters. We therefore wonder what is gained by thinking of these collections as abstractly 'atonal'.[38] Furthermore, Hensel treats some of the harmonic relations in S^2 in a special way, which seems explicitly to negate the possibility of an NRT interpretation.

Example 1.4 Hensel, Piano Trio, Op. 11, i, Allegro molto vivace, bb. 96–112.

After D♭ is first tonicised, the following 'prolongation' unfolds: °T>-°$\cancel{\text{S}}$p=°T-°S^{VII}-D-°T. Two voice exchanges then destabilise the latter harmony. In the last of these, one note of the exchanged dyad, {B♭}, is raised chromatically to {B♮}, yielding a French 6th. This {D♭,F,A♭♭,C♭} chord resolves directly to F minor for a repeat of the antecedent phrase. Crucially, the flattened fifth and seventh of this chord are outside of the hexatonic collection, implied by the background major-third cycle. (The D♭$^6_5$-°F progression in bb. 119–20 and the earlier A-F7 progression in bb. 86–7 also contain notes from outside of this collection.) In other words, when Hensel directly juxtaposes chromatic mediants, the pitch symmetry inherent in the hexatonic scale is purposefully spoiled by extensions. Indeed, it is arguably this 'broken symmetry' that results in the function of the French 6th being both ($\cancel{\text{D}}^{\emptyset}_{5<}$)[°Tp] as well as °$\cancel{\text{F}}^7_{5\flat}$,[39] i.e. the {D♭,G}→{A♭,C} motion suggests a D-T progression in A♭⁺; but the common-tone F facilitates a hearing in which some sense of Tonic is felt throughout. If the previous section demonstrated how pitches that belong to the same hexatonic collection might 'prolong' one another, then notes that perturb hexatonic symmetry – such as the {G}, which forms part of the dominant-functioning tritone with {D♭} – might be thought to make another function audible, highlighting the chord's inherently mixed identity.

It was a recurrent aesthetic issue in mid-to-late-nineteenth-century repertoire that the sequential use of chromatic mediants led to passages that were at one and the same time analytically baffling but nonetheless aurally predictable. The periodic themes that animate the Piano Trio's S-space avoid this pitfall, at least in part, because the resolutions of dominant-functioning chords often cut against the four-square grouping structure of a given phrase. More important, however, is the fact that when the music's hexatonic middle ground is echoed on its surface, Hensel, through her use of extensions and alterations, subtly disrupts the ability of one chord to map perfectly on to another. Implicit in Hensel's approach to chromaticism in 1847, then, is a solution to a problem that plagued many of her New German School successors.

In summary, this chapter has attempted to provide context for the theoretical ideas that characterised Hugo Riemann's career in music theory; we make the case that his function theory provides an essential means of understanding late-nineteenth-century music, particularly the ways in which highly chromatic chords might still be heard to relate (however obliquely) to a tonal centre. While stressing the usefulness of Riemann's system, however, we also acknowledge its shortcomings; the chapter's principal contribution has been to develop a more robust model of harmonic-functional labelling.

Notes

1 See Hugo Riemann, *Dictionary of Music*, trans. J.S. Shedlock (London: Augener, 1896), 146; 276.
2 Alexander Rehding, *Hugo Riemann and the Birth of Musical Thought* (Cambridge: Cambridge University Press, 2002), 41. Rehding cites Carl Friedrich Weitzmann's winning essay in the 1859 *Neue Zeitschrift für Musik* competition, which tasked

authors with explaining contemporary developments in composition, as the source of this quotation, but it is also associated with Max Reger: see Daniel Harrison, *Harmonic Function in Chromatic Music: A Renewed Dualist Theory and an Account of Its Precedents* (Chicago: University of Chicago Press, 1994), 1.

3   Riemann used the epithet 'Social Democrats' to describe theorists such as Melchior Sachs, Albert Hahn, and Heinrich Vincent, who toyed with completely chromatic music theories. See Rehding, *Riemann*, 63.

4   <Angle brackets> are used to indicate ordered pitch successions; {curly brackets} are used to indicate individual pitches or triads.

5   Riemann took this idea to a radical extreme: he would use °C as a shorthand for F minor, for example. While sometimes exploring dualist ideas, we continue to give triads their conventional root designations.

6   This idea is, of course, scientifically bankrupt, but it is easy to see how someone without a scientific background might be duped into believing it. Play a high E on the 12th fret of an acoustic guitar, for example. You will notice that the lowest string will vibrate sympathetically. Surely this string is lower in pitch, and so it cannot be a sympathetic *over*tone that is vibrating: it must be an *under*tone? That's where Riemann went wrong. The lowest string is not vibrating *in its entirety*; only its upper partials resonate with the sounding pitch. That said, it is not true to suggest that the triad exists in nature, either, particularly if one accepts equal temperament. Music theory is a useful fiction, not a scientific fact. If harmonic dualism can be used to explain the coherence of a passage in a striking way, then that is enough.

7   Riemann, *Dictionary of Music*, 146.

8   See also Hugo Riemann, 'The Nature of Harmony' (1882), trans. John Comfort Fillmore and added to his *New Lessons in Harmony* (Philadelphia: T. Presser, 1887), 30. Carl Dahlhaus argues that 'it is in this suspension of diatonicism as the basis of chordal relationships that Riemann saw the distinctive feature of "tonality", as opposed to the "older doctrine of key" founded on the diatonic scale': Carl Dahlhaus, *Studies on the Origin of Harmonic Tonality*, trans. Robert Gjerdingen (Princeton: Princeton University Press, 1990), 11. But the dominance of Weberian ideology was not so easily overcome and Riemann himself seems to have found it difficult to believe his own claims to the contrary. See, for example, Hugo Riemann, *Harmony Simplified; Or, the Theory of the Tonal Functions of Chords* (London: Augener, 1896 [1893]), 145.

9   See David Kopp, *Chromatic Transformations in Nineteenth-Century Music* (Cambridge: Cambridge University Press, 2002), 77.

10 Rehding, *Hugo Riemann*, 51.

11 As Nora Engebretsen explains: 'Whereas Riemann's functional labels identify individual chords' meanings in relation to the tonic, the neo-Riemannian abandonment of tonic reference leaves its "functional" PLR transformations to serve much the same purpose that the *Harmonieschritte* serve in Riemann's theory, namely to provide tonic-blind descriptions of harmonic successions.': 'Neo-Riemannian Perspectives on the *Harmonieschritte*, with a Translation of Riemann's *Systematik der Harmonieschritte*' in *The Oxford Handbook to Neo-Riemannian Music Theories*, eds. Alexander Rehding and Steven Rings (Oxford: Oxford University Press, 2011), 351–81, 354–5. David Lewin saw Riemann's function theory as a nascent form of transformational analysis: 'He [Riemann] did not quite ever realise that he was conceiving "dominant" … as something one *does* to a Klang, to obtain another Klang'. As Kopp has noted, however, Riemann's 1916 operational theory, 'in which he expresses the distance between chord roots as the total product of unit moves by fifth [Q] or major third [T]', is 'closest in nature to Lewin's transformations': see *Chromatic Transformations*, 139; 150. Function theory, by contrast, describes explicitly the *identity* of a single chord (even if it is a 'less pure'

[88] version of an archetype), rather than the relation *between* two chords (the latter task having always been associated with his theory of root-interval progression [154]).

12 *Funktionstheorie* was popularised by Riemann's *Harmony Simplified* (1893), but it was first outlined in the article 'Die Neugestaltung der Harmonielehre', published in Leipzig's *Musikalisches Wochenblatt* in 1891: see Thomas Jul Kirkegaard-Larsen, *Analytical Practices in Western Music Theory: A Comparison and Mediation of Schenkerian and Post-Riemannian Traditions* (Ph.D. diss.: Aarhus University, 2020), 42.

13 As Bryan Hyer puts it, 'For Riemann, functional notation determines the *truth* of a chord and the *truth* of a chord is its function'; 'For Riemann, functional notation indicates the *true* content of the music, the succession of meanings that underlie and accompany the music and guarantee its intelligibility': 'What *Is* a Function?', 109; 111; our emphases.

14 It was Riemann's belief in harmonic dualism that led him to describe the $\hat{5}$-$\hat{6}$ embellishment of any minor triad as a leading-tone transformation. For example, if one were to invert G$^+$ around its fundamental root (i.e. to read the ascending intervals *above* G – namely, a major third and a perfect fifth – as falling *below* G), then °C would be the result (E♭ is a major third *below* G; C a perfect fifth *below* G). If G major was functioning as a dominant, then its third, {B}, would resolve *upwards* to C: i.e. $\hat{7}$-$\hat{8}$. If we understand C minor as the mirror image of G major, then *its* third, {E♭}, would resolve *downwards*, to {D}, effecting a plagal resolution from °C to G$^+$. $\hat{7}$-$\hat{8}$. and ♭$\hat{6}$-$\hat{5}$ can thus be regarded as equal but opposite voice-leading motions. One is 'perfect'; the other, 'plagal'.

15 Riemann introduces this notation in his *Handbuch der Harmonielehre*, 10th ed. (Leipzig: Breitkopf und Härtel, 1929), vii. Much earlier in his career, however, he argued for a conceptually similar labelling – namely, A♭ major = C$^{6♭}_{3♭}$ in C major – in his *Skizze einer neuen Methode der Harmonielehre* (Leipzig: Breitkopf and Härtel, 1880 [1887, 1920]), 67–9. As Kopp notes, however, this notation, which suggests that chromatic mediants are a form of 'tonic', is contradicted by every other statement Riemann makes on the topic in the *Skizze*, in which 'third relations oppose chords to the tonic': see *Chromatic Transformations*, 79; see also 66n15.

16 Riemann, *Handbuch der Harmonielehre*, xvii.

17 On 'scale-denying third chords' ('Skala verleugnenden Terzklänge'), see ibid.

18 As Thomas Christensen notes, 'Riemann is not asking that we consider an A♭ chord to be some chromatically altered form of C major, rather, that we consider both to be representatives and expressions of a dialectically higher class of function called tonic': see 'The Schichtenlehre of Hugo Riemann', *In Theory Only* 6, no. 4 (1982): 42.

19 Riemann, *Harmony Simplified*, 128. Emphasis in the original.

20 Ibid., 70.

21 On the ideas in this subsection, see also J.P.E. Harper-Scott and Oliver Chandler, 'Waltraute's Plaint: Riemannian Tonal Function and Dramatic Narrative', in *Wagner Studies*, ed. Steven Vande Moortele (Cambridge University Press, forthcoming).

22 Hugo Riemann, *Dictionary of Music*, trans. J.S. Shedlock (London: Augener, 1896), 146, 276.

23 That Riemann did not pursue such analyses himself, and eschewed vocal music, is partly to blame for this oversight.

24 Alexander Rehding, 'Tonality between Rule and Repertory; Or, Riemann's Functions—Beethoven's Functions', *Music Theory Spectrum* 33, no. 2 (2011): 109–23, 118.

25 Kenneth Smith, *Desire in Chromatic Harmony: A Psychodynamic Interpretation of Fin de Siècle Tonality* (Oxford: Oxford University Press, 2020), see, particularly, Chapter 1.
26 The enharmonic problems hinted at in Figure 1.2 – 'Wouldn't the final chord be B♭♭♭ rather A♭?' – evaporate if we consider octatonicism, rather than diatonicism, to be this progression's foundation.
27 The principal difference between Smith's and Riemann's theories is that the former prioritises *functional similarity* over *voice-leading proximity* when ascribing harmonic functions to the chords of a hypothetical progression.
28 This is an extrapolation from one of Riemann's own exercises: see *Harmony Simplified; Or, the Theory of the Tonal Functions of Chords* (London: Augener, 1896 [1893]), 80, Example 87(a).
29 Ibid., 74, our italics.
30 A possible exception to this rule is chords resulting from an elided 5-6 suspension. For example, a bassline might arpeggiate a descending F-major chord (C–A–F; S in C major), but the vertical harmonisation for the terminal F might be °D$_5^6$ (i.e. Sp). Often, this is done to avoid parallel fifths, either between the pre-dominant and the preceding tonic (e.g. C/G–F/C) or the proceeding dominant (e.g. F/C–G/D). In such cases, the fifth of the chord is conceptually present (because of the horizontal unfolding) but it is elided with (and replaced by) an actually sounding suspended sixth above the bass.
31 William C. Mickelson, *Hugo Riemann's Theory of Harmony* (London: University of Nebraska Press, 1977), 5.
32 If one disassembles late tonal music into scale-degree assemblages, unmoored from singular, governing chords, then one cannot comprehend in the same detail the ways in which the fundamental building blocks of tonality – T, S, and D functions – might be hollowed out, negated, or clandestinely perpetuated. For an example of the scale-degree approach, see Harrison, *Harmonic Function in Chromatic Music*.
33 Mickelson, *Hugo Riemann's Theory of Harmony*, 25.
34 Adorno, *In Search of Wagner*, 69.
35 See Oliver Chandler, *A Twelve-Tone Repertory for Guitar: Julian Bream and the British Serialists, 1956–1983* (GFA Refereed Monographs, Volume 4: 2023), Chapter 1.
36 Kopp, *Chromatic Transformations*, 6–8.
37 Cohn, *Audacious Euphony*, 23.
38 Ibid., 208.
39 The square brackets indicate an implied (as opposed to present) function.

Bibliography

Adorno, Theodor W. *In Search of Wagner*, translated by Rodney Livingstone. London: Verso, 1981.

Chandler, Oliver. *A Twelve-Tone Repertory for Guitar: Julian Bream and the British Serialists, 1956-1983* (GFA Refereed Monographs, Volume 4, 2023: https://digitalcommons.du.edu/gfamonographs/vol4/iss1/).

Christensen, Thomas. 'The Schichtenlehre of Hugo Riemann', *In Theory Only* 6, no. 4 (1982): 37–44.

Cohn, Richard. *Audacious Euphony: Chromaticism and the Triad's Second Nature*. New York: Oxford University Press, 2012.

Dahlhaus, Carl. *Studies on the Origin of Harmonic Tonality*, translated by Robert Gjerdingen. Princeton: Princeton University Press, 1990.

Engebretsen, Nora. 'Neo-Riemannian Perspectives on the *Harmonieschritte*, with a Translation of Riemann's *Systematik Der Harmonieschritte*', in *The Oxford Handbook to Neo-Riemannian Music Theories*, edited by Edward Golling, and Alexander Rehding, 351–81. Oxford: Oxford University Press, 2011.

Harper-Scott, J.P.E., and Oliver Chandler. 'Waltraute's Plaint: Riemannian Tonal Function and Dramatic Narrative', in *Wagner Studies*, edited by Steven Vande Moortele. Cambridge University Press, forthcoming.

Harrison, Daniel. *Harmonic Function in Chromatic Music: A Renewed Dualist Theory and an Account of Its Precedents*. Chicago: Chicago University Press, 1994.

Hyer, Bryan. 'What Is a Function?' in *The Oxford Handbook to Neo-Riemannian Music Theories*, edited by Edward Gollin, and Alexander Rehding, 92–139. Oxford University Press, 2011.

Kirkegaard-Larsen, Thomas Jul. *Analytical Practices in Western Music Theory: A Comparison and Mediation of Schenkerian and Post-Riemannian Traditions* (Ph.D. diss.). Aarhus University, 2020.

Kopp, David. *Chromatic Transformations in Nineteenth-Century Music*. Cambridge: Cambridge University Press, 2002.

Mickelson, William C. *Hugo Riemann's Theory of Harmony*. London: University of Nebraska Press, 1977.

Rehding, Alexander. *Hugo Riemann and the Birth of Musical Thought*. Cambridge: Cambridge University Press, 2002.

———. 'Tonality Between Rule and Repertory; or, Riemann's Functions—Beethoven's Functions', *Music Theory Spectrum* 33, no. 2 (2011): 109–23.

Riemann, Hugo. *Skizze einer neuen Methode der Harmonielehre* Leipzig: Breitkopf and Härtel, 1880, 1887 [1920].

———. 'The Nature of Harmony', translated by John Comfort Fillmore and added to his *New Lessons in Harmony* (Philadelphia: T. Presser, 1887) 30 (1882).

———. *Harmony Simplified; or, the Theory of the Tonal Functions of Chords*. London: Augener, 1893 [1896].

———. *Handbuch der Harmonielehre*. 10th ed. Leipzig: Breitkopf und Härtel, 1929.

———. *Dictionary of Music*, translated by J. S. Shedlock. London: Augener, 1896.

Smith, Kenneth. *Desire in Chromatic Harmony: A Psychodynamic Interpretation of Fin de Siècle Tonality*. Oxford: Oxford University Press, 2020.

2 Waltraute's Plaint
Riemannian Tonal Function and Dramatic Narrative[1]

In the analysis of late tonal music, approaches that attempt to understand tonal function, on the one hand, and harmonic transformation viewed through a neo-Riemannian lens, on the other, often stand in an uneasy relation. The pleasingly smooth, bidirectional motions between chords in Richard Cohn's 'hexatonic cycles' have encouraged neo-Riemannian theory to bracket out the triumviral power-base of Tonic, Subdominant, and Dominant that in Riemann's hands caused the transformations to emerge in the first place. In the previous chapter, we argued that such bracketing is ultimately wishful thinking: tonality is a system that, like the great socioeconomic, legal, religious, and scientific systems that have endured into the twenty-first century, has an apparently indefatigable ability to subsume anything that might seem to pose a challenge to it back into itself, as a source of further power.[2] In this chapter, however, we aim to explore the advantages of NRT's graphic representations of the triadic universe, while attempting to bring those representations closer to their origins in Riemann's function theory. In doing so, we hope to establish a new theoretical frame for understanding the tonal function of chromatic music.

Our analysis focusses on Waltraute's Plaint: a fellow Valkyrie's narration to Brünnhilde in Wagner's *Götterdämmerung*, Act 1, Scene 3. Already demoted from ruling protagonist to peripheral wanderer in Act 3, Scene 2 of *Siegfried*, Wotan is demoted yet further in this scene: he is represented *in absentia*, with Waltraute functioning as his mouthpiece. And yet, even in (and despite) his exile, the ending of the tetralogy that Waltraute forecasts on her father's behalf does indeed come to pass (even at the continued cost of his own power and presence). It is at this point, we argue, that the character of Wotan becomes synonymous with a new mode of tonality. If he was first represented by the diatonic scale of the Spear motif in *Das Rheingold*, symbolising the tonal laws and authority of the *ancien régime*, he is now associated with an endlessly plastic chromatic tonality that is able to redirect the outbursts of other characters' individuality towards his own plan for the redemption of the world.

Let us introduce Waltraute's Plaint by way of one of the most perceptive analyses to emerge from neo-Riemannian theory in recent years: Graham

DOI: 10.4324/9781003183655-3

Waltraute's Plaint 27

Hunt's close reading of the distortions of the Valhalla motif in *Die Walküre* and *Götterdämmerung*, which itself builds on a pathbreaking essay by David Lewin.³ Example 2.1a shows the original *Rheingold* version of the motif; Example 2.1b shows the corrupted version of this motif that we hear during Wotan's monologue in Act 2, Scene 2 of *Die Walküre*. While the melodic contour is the same, David Lewin noted that its opening chord, f$^{\varnothing 7}$, embeds °G♯ within it; this enters into a Tarnhelm-like relationship with the °E chord that closes the motif (i.e. the two harmonies are connected by an LP transformation). When this motif returns in *Götterdämmerung* (see Example 2.1c), the Tarnhelm reference is further intensified: g♯$^{\varnothing 7}$ (embedding °B) goes to °G; °G then moves to °E♭ (another LP relation), which resolves plagally to B♭⁺. When this progression is repeated in bb. 1242–1245, the last three chords are enharmonically identical to the original Tarnhelm motif (°G♯, °E, B⁺); the only difference is that the open-ended half cadence has become a plagal resolution.

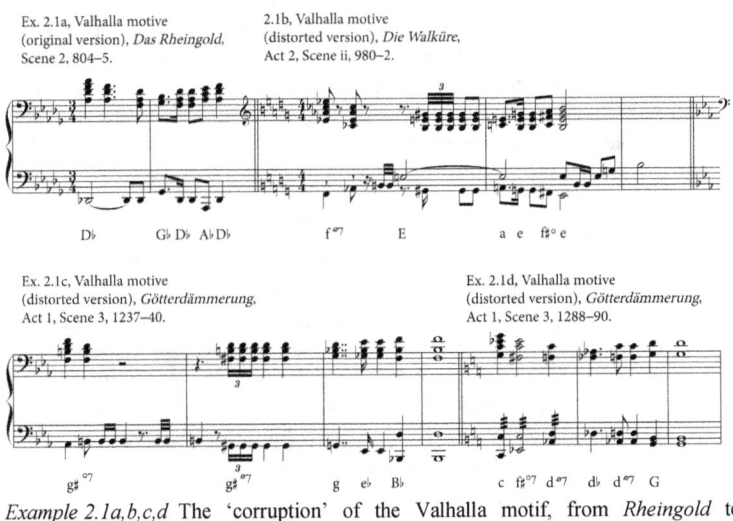

Example 2.1a,b,c,d The 'corruption' of the Valhalla motif, from *Rheingold* to *Götterdämmerung*.

Building on Lewin's original insights, Hunt argues that we might understand the relationship of g♯$^{\varnothing 7}$ to °G more precisely in terms of what he calls a '*Leittonwechsel* split' plus a parallel transformation: G♯ and F♯ 'fuse' (the inverse of 'splitting') to G♮ (S*$_L$); the resultant G-major chord is then modally altered (P). This finely honed characterisation, which is able to accommodate all of the chords' sounding pitches, facilitates new insights later in the Plaint. In m. 1288, for instance, the move from d$^{\varnothing 7}$ to °D♭ and back (see Example 2.1d) can be profitably understood as a further intensification of the underlying

PL transformations of bb. 1237–41. Rather than $S*_L P$, LP, we now have $S*_L P$, $PS*_L$. The music is becoming more dissonant and chordally enriched, while still remaining recognisably Valhalla-like.

The merging of motivic identities (Valhalla and Tarnhelm) here, so well elucidated by neo-Riemannian theory, reveals something essential about the drama. As Hunt puts it:

> The construction of Valhalla itself led to the corrupt state of affairs surrounding the cursed ring and will later lead to the evil plot of Alberich's son, Hagen, whose scheme centres around the Tarnhelm. These dramatic threads come together in Wotan's outburst in *Die Walküre*, when he resignedly presages his ultimate destruction and seems to realise its ultimate source.[4]

But there is another aspect of this scene that a neo-Riemannian perspective does not capture so easily: namely, its overall tonality, and the meaning of that tonality in the context of the dramatic whole. Through a return to Riemann, this chapter looks to model a new theory of chromatic harmony that can make such meanings clearer. First, however, we must examine another facet of Wotan's – and Valhalla's – musico-dramatic function in the tetralogy. Whereas Hunt emphasises the god's ailing powers, we wish to highlight the dialectically opposite situation, in which Wotan's influence grows, even as it appears to diminish.

Wotan's Will, Tonality, and Rhetorical Dialectics

Pace Adorno, we take one of the founding principles of the *Ring* to be the transubstantiation of nature into history.[5] If *Das Rheingold* represents, at some level, the mythologisation of a declining but not yet moribund bourgeois society – a contingent political reality elevated to the level of a universal truth – then by the end of *Götterdämmerung* that contingency has been revealed: first nature becomes second nature. The transformation of Wotan's power and status in *Götterdämmerung* – illustrated by the transformations of the Valhalla motif, associated with his 'abstract presence or influence'[6] – bears the trace of this overall trajectory. On the one hand, the motivic corruption Hunt identifies represents the waning of his influence: the old god gives way both to the 'man of the future', Siegfried, and to his own daughter. But on the other, the Valhalla motive's myriad guises, particularly in Act 2, Scene 2 in *Die Walküre* and Waltraute's Plaint in *Götterdämmerung*, represent the ubiquity and elasticity of his influence. When Brünnhilde burns down Valhalla, it is partly because Wotan has willed it so: note the parallelism between Act 1, Scene 3, bb. 1305–9, in which Waltraute describes Wotan's hope that his ravens may bring him good tidings – that the ring has been returned to the Rhinemaidens – and Act 3, Scene 3, bb. 1359–63, in which Brünnhilde makes good on that hope, instructing the ravens to return to their master with news that he may now rest. When Wotan confides in Waltraute, he knows that the restoration of the ring to its rightful keepers will not restore his own power (his spear has already been destroyed by Siegfried); and yet, it is only through his own initiating act of will – his decision to bring freedom into the world, in the form both of Siegfried and Brünnhilde – that this situation will ultimately be actualised. In other words, to scorn and 'put at nought' the 'body and its imperatives' in the name of freedom, Wotan must do what no immortal can: namely, to accept mortality.[7] He does this 'first through his proxy Brünnhilde, and then through his own act of renunciation at the start of *Siegfried* Act 3.[8] His own failure becomes, through a dialectical sleight of hand, his crowning achievement.

Valhalla is, in one sense, the dream of a bourgeois home without conflict, but Wotan ultimately recognises that this dream cannot be realised in a fallen world.[9] By both destroying and beautifying Valhalla at the very end of the cycle, Wagner keeps alive the ideal that Wotan dreamed of, while avoiding fetishizing that ideal in the form of a sordid object from the present situation.[10] To achieve this profound effect, Wagner quotes an earlier version of the Valhalla motif from Act 1, Scene 3 (bb. 1259–67): Waltraute relates to Brünnhilde how Wotan had assembled Valhalla's citizens around his throne, the pomp of the music an ironic counterpoint to the fear and anxiety the heroes felt as Wotan sat silently, preparing for the fortress' immolation. The sheer dynamic and textural weight of this motif's seemingly affirmative re-presentation in *Götterdämmerung*'s final pages (bb. 1561–90) seem to indicate that Waltraute's (and Wotan's) hopes for the redemption of Valhalla have been fulfilled; but the chromatic transformation of its constituent harmonies, suggesting foreground tonicizations of C major, D phrygian, D♭ minor, and G♭ major, before settling back into its original D♭ major, suggest simultaneously and paradoxically the destruction of said institution: the hollowing out of its fundamental tonality. Art cannot provide an explicit image of utopia. The possible 'nature' or form of the utopian world that does not yet exist can be imitated only by the determinate negation of the falsely naturalised culture that *does* exist.

The dialectic just described – between Wotan's waning influence and his latent omnipotence; between the dismantling of Valhalla and the expression of its ineradicable potential as an ideal – is arguably best reflected in the strained tonalities that contextualise, and thus inflect the meaning of, the Valhalla motif. Wagner's tonality is both coercive – one cannot escape its clutches – and emancipatory, insofar as its very elasticity and capaciousness expose the lack of a *ground* for tonality: that is, tonality does not exist as a natural principle, but as a historically contingent ideology to which harmonic monads are subject (with the proviso that they *might not be* if they were to exist in a different world-historical situation). For this reason, tonality may one day be overthrown, even if such an overthrow, by existing as part of a future present, will be condemned to perpetuate that same present – hence Wagner's often-remarked-on pessimism.[11]

It is at this point that our argument returns to its dialogue with Adorno: 'Even the entanglement of world history in myth in the *Ring* is something more than the expression of a determinist metaphysics; it also makes possible a critique of a badly determined world [e.g. by laying bear the ideological structuring of that world]'.[12] On the one hand, tonality in *Götterdämmerung* is literally fathomless, because it has no ground: keys no longer have stable associations with singular characters, as they did in *Das Rheingold*[13]; there is no associative *Ur*-structure to be composed-out. And yet this groundlessness is the condition of possibility for the music to exist, the music's unfolding merely *as if* it had a ground – as if, that is, it were grounded in the way that the tonal art of Bach or Mozart is grounded. The 'emancipation of the dominant' in the late nineteenth century – whereby, in Jim Samson's words, 'the higher numbered dominant-quality dissonances [...] achieved harmonic status, with resolution delayed or omitted completely' – communicates the passing of the old tonal gods.[14] The freedom of Wagner's harmony is a nullity, granted by the impotence of the old system of tonality (the gods of Valhalla, the *ancien régime*). And yet this freedom has not (yet) given up the projection of tonal meaning. To put the case in Heideggerian terms, in retaining its focus on triads – each of which is explicable in a triumviral tonal power structure of Tonic, Subdominant, and Dominant – *Götterdämmerung* 'projects itself upon the possibilities into which it is thrown', i.e. it projects for itself a form that makes use of the tonal possibilities of the triadic language which historical circumstance provides, even in the absence of a functioning tonal structure.[15] In other words, 'Music' does not yet know what to do with its own freedom, and reactively attempts to act on the basis of its old, pre-Revolutionary 'throwing'. The language of *Götterdämmerung* hovers between a nullified grounding in tonality and an entirely new conception of musical space – but it never crosses the line, and it always returns to the nullity of familiar tonal ground. In much the same way, Wotan's will in this last opera of the tetralogy is both impotent and all powerful: physically absent but symbolically ubiquitous. It is exactly this dialectic, both dramatic and musical, that we argue that neo-Riemannian theory cannot explain because of its methodological commitment to relativism: e.g. any harmonic choice within a given symmetrical structure has the same meaning as any other; Wotan has no more or less power than any other character.

Hunt's analysis provides an excellent starting point from which to begin testing the veracity of our proposition. Hunt understands his $S^*_L P$ transformations, for example, to take place in a 'chromatic zone', 'which carries larger function' in relation to the 'diatonic zones' by which it is bookended.[16] 'Approaching the surface of the music from this [perspective] avoids the pitfalls of "eliminating" surface chromatic details through reduction while still situating the chromaticism within its diatonic surroundings'.[17]

While Hunt argues that this perspective does not imply 'a strict boundary between diatonicism and chromaticism'[18] – that is, between a hierarchical space and a relativistic one – it does rely implicitly on something like Cohn's code-switching model, outlined in the final two chapters of his book, *Audacious Euphony*. Cohn argues that individual triads and seventh chords function as 'magical worm holes ... that inhabit two distinct spaces ... "without apparent conflict"'.[19] These syntactic spaces work according to different logics: diatonic, functional progression in the first case (i.e. tonality); and smooth voice-leading transformation in the second (i.e. non-tonality).[20] 'Tonality', on this model, is based on acoustic principles in which the major tonic triad and its transposition by ascending and descending fifth (the next strongest interval in the overtone series and its inversion) are the primary generators. 'Non-tonal', pan-triadic, or tetrachordal progressions, by contrast, treat triads (or seventh chords) as 'nearly even' perturbations of totally symmetrical augmented triads (or fully diminished seventh chords). Consonant chords might thus be said to have two general proclivities, depending on whether we think of them in terms of their 'appellative' or 'set-class' properties. In the former case, chords act as their conventional names would imply: 'E♭ major' will be potentially associated with a particular scale step in a particular key. In the latter case, the more neutral set-class designation, e.g. [037], brackets out ideas of root or key association, opening the door (for those who choose to walk through it) to a world in which one chord may move smoothly to any other in a chromatic system of tight voice leading.[21]

Surely this model is implicitly dialectical? In his discussion of the transformation of a {158} trichord to {148} in the third movement of Schubert's ninth symphony (bb. 117–28), for example, Cohn suggests that, while the 'C♯/D♭' chord 'still retains its forked syntactic and appellative residues in diatonic space [first as a Neapolitan chord in C major, then as the *Leittonwechsel* of a dominant chord in D minor] what comes to the fore as syntactic driver is the minimal change relation between adjacent triads: each motion only requires a semitonal motion'.[22] The packaging of this statement might appear dialectical, but it ultimately dissimulates a binary mode of thought. Ontologically speaking, {158} and {148} manifest here as part of a hexatonic space; they are *not* D♭⁺ and °C♯ chords, despite their appearance: i.e. they 'belong' to a scale that is fundamentally symmetrical, obviating the need for enharmonic distinction. While a composer might pivot between acoustic and smooth voice-leading worlds through the hidden seam of a given consonant chord, the systems themselves (as opposed to the objects that populate those systems) are ultimately 'incommensurate'.[23]

For there to be a genuinely dialectical understanding of tonality, one must consider the meanings that chromatic, smooth voice-leading progressions might have from a tonal standpoint, and *vice versa*. What exists on one side of the 'systemic' divide must exist simultaneously (albeit differently, perhaps even paradoxically) on the other. This is the basis of Wagner's own theory of 'rhetorical dialectics'.[24] Tonality exists as a natural principle, but 'a poetic-dramatic text could serve as a pretext for departing from such conventionalised formal principles — offering a poetic license, as it were, for their transgression, and at the same time explaining it'.[25] But such departures would not have the special meanings that are immanent within them if they did not sublate – that is, carry within themselves as a negation – the tonal norms they

32 Waltraute's Plaint

trespass against. Rather than being coincidental epiphenomena, these norms and their immanent negation are *essential* to a given progression's meaning. Where music ends and drama begins cannot be pinpointed.

Lunar Tonality

Chapter 1 represented our attempt to fortify *Funktionstheorie*. That done, we are in a position to map the chromatic-diatonic universe that emerges. Because of the generally hexatonic proclivities of Waltraute's Plaint, we have replaced Cohn's chord designations from his hexatonic cycles diagram with some of Riemann's functions, exaggerating the link that Cohn occasionally draws himself (see Figure 2.1).[26] Each circle has a predominantly tonic, subdominant, dominant, or mixed function, as indicated by the 'T', 'S', 'D', and 'Sp/D' at their centres. For each of the principal tonal functions, which are shown in the top, left, and right circles, there is a motion from relative diatonic strength to one of relative chromatic strength.

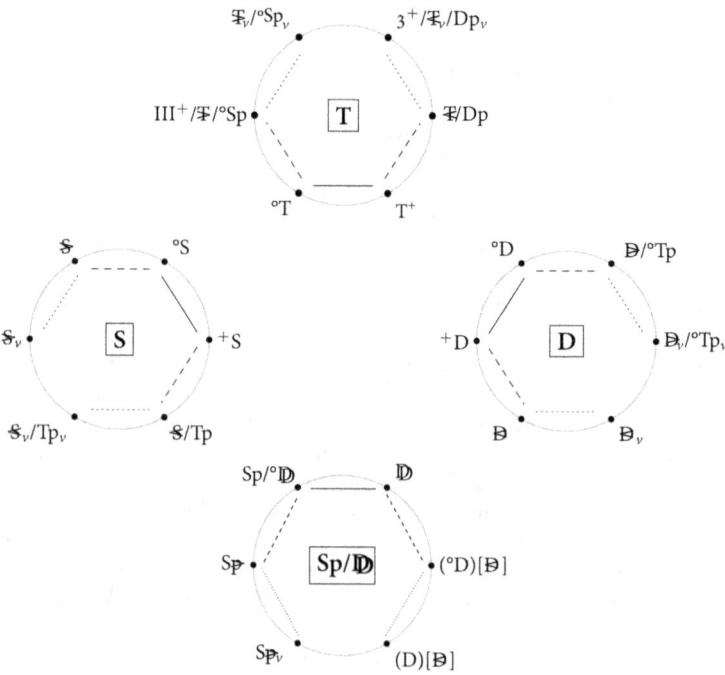

Figure 2.1 A model of Lunar Tonality, composed of Functional Moons.

In the top circle, the major and minor tonics sit at the bottom, linked by a solid line that indicates the strength of these two functions in respect of the tonic. Each of these tonics, major and minor, has its *Leittonwechsel*. In certain contexts (particularly octatonic ones: see Constraint No. 1, described in Chapter 1), those chords can have alternative functions, which are therefore also given on the circle; but in Waltraute's Plaint (as already outlined), it is a hexatonic logic that is most in evidence. These functions, relatively diatonic, are connected to the strongest tonic functions with a dashed line, indicating their strong but slightly attenuated tonal function. Beyond them, connected by dotted lines, are the variants of the *Leittonwechsel*.

Instead of the relativistic space of the normal hexatonic conception, this tonic circle is now laden with tonal meaning. Cohn tends to play down this potential, but we want to lay stress on it. At the solid-line face, looking towards the centre of the whole diagram, are the strongest tonic functions. As motion continues towards the other side of the circle, tonal function becomes more chromatic, requiring one or two chromatic alterations of the original tonic triad. In contrast to the hexatonic perspective, this diagram focusses attention *both* on the chromatic *and* on the diatonic elements of the tonal music at hand. The other circles follow the pattern of the tonic circle.

These four circles might usefully be imagined to be 'moons' of the Planet Tonality, which is conceptually located somewhere at the centre.[27] The faces they present towards their governing planet are, like the lighted side of Earth's moon, the best-known features of these moons, i.e. the most diatonic chords in tonal music. The harmonies at the 'back' of each circle might thus be conceived as lying on the 'dark side' of each moon, which produce the most 'alien' tonal effects. And yet, whether they are diatonic/light-side, or chromatic/dark-side, each of these harmonies has the potential to move in lunar orbits that make more or less immediate functional sense. Encultured listeners to late tonal music, whether members of the general public or music theory students beginning their training, frequently say that they feel a piece is tonal without being able to comprehend its seemingly inexplicable chord progressions. Indeed, this functional reappropriation of Cohn's hexatonic system remains faithful to that encultured but as-yet-untrained hearing, and sets up the possibility of explaining the duality of this music: the strong double sense that it is tonal, and that it is complex or even weird in its treatment of tonality.

Dark-Side Functions in Waltraute's Plaint

Let us see this model of tonal space in action. Example 2.2 reproduces Waltraute's Plaint, from bb. 1234–55. (The reader is encouraged to relate the various Riemannian annotations to the lunar diagram in Figure 2.1.) This is the same music surveyed in Hunt's analysis, and with which this chapter began. From Riemann's perspective, which disavows diminished triads, the chords in bb. 1237–39 would be interpreted as $Đ^{9>}$, $°S^{VII}$, and $\mathbf{S}_v$: a move from a fairly clear, 'light-side' dominant function to an obscure, 'dark-side' subdominant function. (Tonal functions are indicated below each system, and the lines grouping together harmonies with T, S, and D functions indicate larger *functional fields*, which hold the tonality in place.)

Example 2.2 Vocal score reduction of Waltraute's Plaint, bb. 1234–55, with Riemannian annotations.

The function of the third chord of the distorted Valhalla motive (°S̷ᵥ) is clarified with the next chord in b. 1239 (𝄞), which requires only two stops clockwise around the subdominant moon to reach °S. From there Wagner effects a *Seitenwechsel*, a dualist swing between chords that both have B♭ as their prime (read under- and overtonally, respectively, °B♭–B♭⁺) to cadence °E♭ to B♭⁺. The latter, as well as being the *Seitenwechsel* of the °S, is on the opposite side of the tonic moon from its starting point of °F♯. A 'hexatonic pole', in Cohn's terms, this chord receives its own Ð⁹˃ in the next two bars, for the start of the second distorted Valhalla motive.²⁸ This progression then becomes the basis, albeit constantly reconfigured, for the remainder of the passage. (The opening of *Tristan und Isolde*, with its varied repetitions of the Tristan chord and its resolution, is, in fact, not wholly unrelated to what occurs here if we parse the fully diminished chords as corrupted dominant sevenths that move 'smoothly' to half-diminished sevenths.)

Three times we hear the distorted Valhalla motive, and three times a very similar sequence of chords is heard, each 'strange' in its relation to the overall tonic (°A in *Tristan und Isolde*, °F♯ here), but each necessarily contributing to a projection of the tonic – Wotan's will – across the entire passage. In Waltraute's Plaint, the first distorted Valhalla chord (bb. 1237, 1242, and 1252) enters as a dominant ninth function of the preceding tonic harmony, which then subsequently becomes S°ᵛᴵᴵ, ambiguated by the subsequent move to a more dark-side subdominant via the split leading tone Hunt identifies, which resolves the seventh but places chordal function at a further remove.

On its first appearance, Ð⁹˃ is a dominant of the passage's overall °T; the second time (b. 1242), the dominant relation is to (𝔗ᵥ, B♭⁺; and on its third appearance, the harmony is still more intense: it is the dominant ninth of the major-dominant *Leittonwechsel* (Ð⁹˃ [𝄞]), *a transformation of the preceding* (𝄞) (i.e. °D♯) – an extremely remote function.²⁹ Rather than resolving directly to the tonic, the chord proceeds to a point of rest on a 'dissonant' triad, in a broadly similar way to the Tristan chord. Specifically, on each occasion the 'resolving' chord is reinterpreted as the major-subdominant *Leittonwechsel* of a new plagal progression: it moves twice (𝄞 –°S–°T (bb. 1239 and 1254), once (𝄞–°S–T⁺ (b. 1244)).

On the first occurrence of the motive the final tonic-related harmony (𝔗ᵥ, B♭⁺, three chromatic changes from the tonic °F♯), feels disjunct, remote from the starting point, but recognizably a tonal waystation on account both of the strong plagal 'feel' of its cadence and of the fact that the harmony comes to rest here, signalling a brief 'close' of some kind. When it then subsequently receives its own dominant, however, the sense that this chord, like the one with which we began, might function 'as a tonic' is reconfirmed, but the transformation of that dominant into a *Leittonwechsel* of the following subdominant progression effects, for the second time in this passage, an uncanny gesture of decentring the sense of developing tonic. Yet this uncanniness is ephemeral: the new 'tonic', (C♭, S overall) is chewed over, with shifting chromatic alterations to its seventh, fifth, and third, for the next five and a half bars, as Waltraute relates how Wotan commands the destruction of the World Ash Tree, which will bring the time of the gods to its end. On the word 'Weltesche' Waltraute sings a descending arpeggio in °E♭, which swiftly moves to an intensified (D⁹ᐳ)[D] at the start of the final Valhalla cadence – final not only in this passage, but in the sense that she is telling of the fortress's imminent destruction. Sounding on its own, without a vocal part to distract the audience's attention, the Valhalla motive follows its strange-sounding S–°S–T motion for a final time, now closing back to the diatonic tonic (enharmonically spelled as G♭ *major*) in which the passage had begun. This T subsequently continues for the next thirty-three bars, cadencing half way along its course with a beautiful restoration of the original Valhalla-motive cadence (in bb. 1267–70), as Waltraute's dreadful prognosis turns to fond memory of the Valhalla she and Brünnhilde had once served.

This passage is one of the more striking of *Götterdämmerung*'s highly chromatic treatments of familiar leitmotives in the context of a very free tonality. And yet it demonstrates very clearly how, despite the initial difficulty of comprehension, music of this chromatic richness, which slides decadently around the hexatonic moons – arguably reflecting the attenuation of Wotan's will – nevertheless projects tonal function. Despite appearances, Wotan's will (reflected by and synonymous with some form of tonic) will be manifested. Through these bars we effectively hear two iterations of a °T–D⁺–°S–°T cadence (indicated by the tonal field brackets beneath the score).[30] On the face of it, this might seem both a stunningly disappointing and an implausible conclusion, because it suggests that Wagner's advanced chromatic style is considerably more conventional than musicologists and music theorists are accustomed to thinking, even when they believe the music is organised around a tonal centre. How can such a perspective be squared with a century of Wagnerian criticism focussing on that which is musically errant? Ernst Kurth's writings (here paraphrased by Cohn) exemplify the latter position:

> [Wagner's] chromatic progressions, particularly those that involved root relations by third, introduced rifts, wedges, and fissures into the fabric of tonality. [...] When concatenated with sufficient intensity and persistence, such absolute progressions bring about 'the total disruption of the original embracing tonal unity'.[31]

This kind of binary thinking does not do justice to the subtlety of Wagner's dialecticism. 'Fissures' are introduced because of their correlation to a dramatic (as opposed to an autonomously musical) object; but this dramatic choice only carries the meaning that it does because Wagner's mature chromatic style represents a determinate negation of the existing musical world, of tonality, which does exist (but not, crucially, a presentation of a post-tonal utopian reality, which does not exist). *Determinate negation is the truth content of Wagnerian functional ambiguity, of its unconcealing/concealing 'dark-side' functions*. But this does not, *pace* Kurth, amount to 'the total disruption of the original embracing tonal unity'.[32] Indeed, on Adorno's view, 'the dissonances [in Wagner's phrasing] have assumed the character of sovereign subjectivity vis-à-vis the resolutions: they protest against the right of a social authority to make the rules'.[33]

The dark-side functions of Waltraute's Valhalla cadences, such as its first arrival on $\mathfrak{T}_v$, let alone the more adventurous $\mathfrak{D}^{9>}[\mathfrak{D}]$ at the beginning of the final Valhalla motive, are *at a remove from but only partly emancipated from* their normative functions. The chords do not abandon function entirely for at least two good reasons. First, they have clear short-range functions: i.e. as the culmination of the local $\mathfrak{S}$ -°S-T motion employed in each of the Valhalla cadences. And second, the long-range functions that they transform do, in every case, follow a sequential logic to unfold bilateral cadences in the way earlier and simpler tonal music had long done. They therefore do not establish a second kind of syntax in which function is no longer a totalising force in tonal music; rather, they 'protest against the right of a social authority to make the rules', while continuing, ultimately, to obey them, and through the critical nature of their obedience to point to what would have to be eradicated were a new world to be realised. As a consequence, in the Wagnerian idiolect, functions such as $\mathfrak{T}$ or $\mathfrak{T}_v$ can seem to hold as great a 'tonic' functional sway as T⁺ itself, of which these chords are simply *Leittonwechsel* and variant transformations. They simply subject that tonic, that musical symbol of a social ideology – Wotan's will, bourgeois norms – to a determinate negation, to question the form of society that assumes as its right the control of individual subjects in the interests of a hegemonic centre.

Notes

1 This chapter presents a varied form of an argument we have also made in *Wagner Studies*, ed. Steven Vande Moortele (Cambridge: Cambridge University Press, in press).
2 Readers might want some form of clarification here: are tonality and capitalism really coeval, as we have intimated? Tonality was first *theorised* in the nineteenth century. Arguably, then, its existence as an idea overlaps with the development of a post–French Revolution proprietarianism into capitalism proper, catalysed by the growth of heavy industry and international finance (see Piketty 2020). Surely the musical behaviours that the concept of tonality codified, however, were a century older, at the very least? There are two things to say, here: (1) It is often arbitrary to search for an absolute beginning for historical phenomena such as tonality or capitalism: they manifest as constellations that take their shape from related but often somewhat disjointed data, lacking a singular cause; and (2) Before the nineteenth century, with its greater awareness of tonality's contingencies – prompted by

research into musics of the past and of other cultures in a wider colonial economy, as well as the experiments of the New German School – what we now call tonality might well have been understood simply as what music *was* (see Christensen 2019). If one learnt composition in a small village in Bavaria, for example, music's possibilities would have been set out by one's organ teacher or choir master. Likely, nothing was imaginable beyond this. It was only when composers came to understand tonality as contingent, and thus tried to move past it, that its status as an ideology (as opposed to a mere stylistic default) began. Ultimately, though, tonality and capitalism were concurrent in the nineteenth century, whether or not their beginnings can be mapped onto one another. (We might not always be able to pinpoint when we contracted an illness; it is the *ex post facto* symptoms that alert us.)

3   Graham G. Hunt, 'David Lewin and Valhalla Revisited: New Approaches to Motivic Corruption in Wagner's Ring Cycle', *Music Theory Spectrum* 29, no. 2 (2007): 177–96; David Lewin, 'Some Notes on Analyzing Wagner', *19th Century Music*, 16, no. 1 (1992): 49–58.
4   Hunt, 'David Lewin and Valhalla', 180.
5   Theodor W. Adorno, *In Search of Wagner*, trans. Rodney Livingstone (London: Verso, 1981).
6   Hunt, 'David Lewin and Valhalla', 177.
7   Roger Scruton, *The Ring of Truth: The Wisdom of Wagner's* Ring of the Nibelung (London: Penguin, 2017), 258.
8   Ibid., 258.
9   In reality, of course, there is much conflict between Wotan and Fricka in Act 2 of *Die Walküre*, and the institution's very foundation involved Freia's debasement.
10 On this point, we were much influenced by Arnold Whittall, *The Wagner Style: Close Readings and Critical Perspectives* (London: Plumbago Books, 2015), 141–61.
11 Such pessimism is often associated with Wagner's discovery of Schopenhauer; but Wagner himself noted that, even during his utopian anarchist phase, the meaning of the *Ring*'s ending had seemed to forecast his later Schopenhauerian turn: 'I looked at my Nibelung poems and recognised to my amazement that the very things I now found so unpalatable in [Schopenhauer's] theory were already long familiar to me in my own poetic conception. Only now did I understand my own Wotan myself…', cited in Bryan Magee, *Wagner and Philosophy* (London: Penguin Books, 2000), 179.
12 Adorno, *In Search of Wagner*, 130.
13 See Robert Bailey, 'The Structure of the "Ring" and Its Evolution', *19th-Century Music* 1, no. 1 (1977): 48–61, 54n10.
14 Jim Samson, *Music in Transition: A Study of Tonal Expression and Atonality, 1900–1920* (London: J.M. Dent & Sons Ltd, 1977), 146–7. This process mirrors and develops the interval of the seventh's earlier change in character, from a contrapuntal dissonance to a quasi-harmonic consonance, at the beginning of the nineteenth century.
15 Martin Heidegger, *Being and Time: A Translation of "Sein und Zeit,"* trans. Joan Stambaugh (New York, 1996), 262–3.
16 Hunt, 'David Lewin and Valhalla', 182. See, for example, Example 7(d), 188.
17 Ibid., 181, n. 3.
18 Ibid., 180.
19 Richard Cohn, *Audacious Euphony: Chromaticism and the Triad's Second Nature* (New York: Oxford University Press, 2012), 173–4.
20 Ibid., 205–8. For specific use of the term 'atonal', see 208.
21 Ibid., 204–5.
22 Ibid., 198.
23 Ibid., 199.

24 This term comes from Wagner's 1879 essay 'On the Application of Music to the Drama'. See Richard Wagner, *Richard Wagner's Prose Works, Vol. VI: Religion and Art*, trans. William Ashton Ellis (London: Kegan Paul, Trench, Trübner & Co, Ltd., 1897), 173–91.
25 Thomas Grey, *Wagner's Musical Prose* (Cambridge: Cambridge University Press, 1995), 305.
26 See Richard Cohn, 'As Wonderful as Star Clusters: Instruments for Gazing at Tonality in Schubert', *19th-Century Music* (1999): 213–32. It is noteworthy, however, that, in a later publication, Cohn acknowledged the entirely heuristic nature of his tonal analogies in the former article: 'If we are attracted to functions primarily because they encourage us to bundle musical events into coherent trajectories, such as the departure → overshoot → return scheme documented here, then they are dispensable', *Audacious Euphony*, 128. While Cohn acknowledges the viability of interpreting hexatonic progressions functionally here, he does not see chromatic functionality as an essential part of Schubert's style. It is merely one mode of post-modern 'knowing', rather than (as for us) a necessary horizon of historical meaning.
27 This astronomical terminology is, to some extent, anticipated in Julian Horton, 'Form and Orbital Tonality in the Finale of Bruckner's Seventh Symphony', *Music Analysis* 37, no. iii (2018): 271–309 and Kelvin H. Lee, 'Formalising Star Clusters: Sonata Process and Breakthrough Function in the Adagio of Mahler's Tenth Symphony', *Music Analysis* 40, no. ii (2021): 178–226. For these authors, however, each chord of a hexatonic system counts as 'one entire classically diatonic tonal universe [i.e. a particular 'orbit']. [...] Inter-orbital relationships, although logical, are essentially disjunctive: when we shift between them, *we toggle competing systems, which behave like contiguous but dissociated tonal dimensions*': see Horton, 'Orbital Tonality', 280, our italics. For us, by contrast, there is no toggling: hexatonic triads, while more distant from a potential centre of tonal gravity than most diatonic chords, are still fundamentally oriented by its gravitational field.
28 The strikethrough indicates that the fundamental root of the chord has been omitted; ⁹⁾ indicates the flattening of its ninth.
29 The (round brackets) indicate an applied function: in this case, the dominant-seventh flattened-ninth *of* 𝄐. The [square brackets] indicate a function that is implied by the music, but which does not materialise.
30 Riemann suggests that 'the clang successions T-S-D-T and °T-°S-°D-T° are ... typical for harmonic motions in general; they are so-called *complete (bilateral) cadences*': see Riemann, *Harmony Simplified*, 44. But it is perfectly normal for these to become modally mixed, and his use of a +dominant inflection creates a 'yearning straining upwards into the bright domain of major relations' (ibid.) that makes perfect sense in the context of Waltraute's plea to Brünnhilde.
31 Cohn, *Audacious Euphony*, 10, quoting Ernst Kurth in Lee Rothfarb (trans. and ed.), *Ernst Kurth: Selected Writings* (Cambridge: Cambridge University Press, 1991), 120.
32 Ibid.
33 Adorno, *In Search of Wagner*, 54–5.

Bibliography

Adorno, Theodor W. *In Search of Wagner* translated by Rodney Livingstone. London: Verso, 1981.

Bailey, Robert. 'The Structure of the 'Ring' and Its Evolution', *19th-Century Music* 1, no. 1 (1977): 48–61.

Christensen, Thomas. *Stories of Tonality in the Age of François-Joseph Fétis*. Chicago: University of Chicago Press, 2019.

Cohn, Richard. 'As Wonderful as Star Clusters: Instruments for Gazing at Tonality in Schubert', *19th-Century Music* 22, no. 3 (1999): 213–32.

———. *Audacious Euphony: Chromaticism and the Triad's Second Nature*. New York: Oxford University Press, 2012.

Grey, Thomas. *Wagner's Musical Prose*. Cambridge: Cambridge University Press, 1995.

Harper-Scott, J. P. E., and Oliver Chandler. 'Waltraute's Plaint: Riemannian Tonal Function and Dramatic Narrative', in *Wagner Studies*, edited by Steven Vande Moortele. Cambridge University Press, in press.

Heidegger, Martin. *Being and Time: A Translation of "Sein und Zeit"*, translated by Joan Stambaugh. New York: SUNY, 1996.

Horton, Julian. 'Form and Orbital Tonality in the Finale of Bruckner's Seventh Symphony', *Music Analysis* 37, no. iii (2018): 271–309.

Hunt, Graham G. 'David Lewin and Valhalla Revisited: New Approaches to Motivic Corruption in Wagner's Ring Cycle', *Music Theory Spectrum* 29, no. 2 (2007): 177–96.

Lee, Kelvin H. 'Formalising Star Clusters: Sonata Process and Breakthrough Function in the Adagio of Mahler's Tenth Symphony', *Music Analysis* 40, no. ii (2021): 178–226.

Lewin, David. 'Some Notes on Analyzing Wagner', *19th Century Music* 16, no. 1 (1992): 49–58.

Magee, Bryan. *Wagner and Philosophy*. London: Penguin Books, 2000.

Piketty, Thomas. *Capital and Ideology*, translated by Arthur Goldhammer. London: Harvard University Press, 2020.

Riemann, Hugo. *Harmony Simplified; or, the Theory of the Tonal Functions of Chords* London: Augener, 1896 [1893].

Rothfarb, Lee (trans. and ed.). *Ernst Kurth: Selected Writings*. Cambridge: Cambridge University Press, 1991.

Samson, Jim. *Music in Transition: A Study of Tonal Expression and Atonality, 1900–1920*. London: J M Dent & Sons Ltd, 1977.

Scruton, Roger. *The Ring of Truth: The Wisdom of Wagner's Ring of the Nibelung*. London: Penguin, 2017.

Wagner, Richard. *Richard Wagner's Prose Works, Vol. VI: Religion and Art*, translated by William Ashton Ellis. London: Kegan Paul, Trench, Trübner & Co, Ltd., 1897.

Whittall, Arnold. *The Wagner Style: Close Readings and Critical Perspectives*. London: Plumbago Books, 2015.

3 Two Nineteenth-Century Examples of Hexatonic-Diatonic Tonal Function

Many examples of music from the early nineteenth to the mid-twentieth centuries could be adduced to show what kinds of analytical insights emerge when the hexatonic and diatonic aspects of tonal functions are drawn in the way modelled in the previous chapter; but, before turning to the complex functional *fields*, as we shall call the longer-range projections of highly chromatic tonal function in later chapters, we shall here offer two quite brief examples – one taken from Beethoven, one from Brahms – that give an indication of the different 'flavours' of tonality that emerge when the relation between these two systems and the trajectory across the tonal moons takes on different forms. In both cases, chromatic motion operates relatively clearly in support of a cadentially closed modulatory motion, but in cases like the Brahms example, there has been a tendency to downplay, or even tacitly to ignore, the modulatory and cadential functions in order to focus relativistically on harmonic shapes that emerge during the most concentrated chromatic passages.

Beethoven, Piano Sonata in C Minor, Op. 10, No. 1

Figure 3.1 graphs the harmonic trajectory from b. 31 (the start of the transition) to b. 55 (the start of the secondary theme) of Beethoven's Piano Sonata in C minor, Op. 10, No. 1, which is shown in Example 3.1, along with some analytical notation that we shall shortly explain. After a strong, 'C-minor-mood' primary theme presenting a thirty-bar tonic field with recourse only to D^+ and $°T$ functions, the transition moves immediately flatwards, ultimately resulting in a full close in the sonata's secondary key, $E♭^+$ (globally Tp). The passage begins on a single {$E♭$}, a note that implies a dominant function in the key of $A♭^+$, a chord onto which it unfurls downwards by b. 36 (see the motion from T, on the top moon, to S, on the left-hand moon in Figure 3.1, which begins the motion this analysis will chart). This opening gesture, which represents an implied T-S in the ultimate key, is indicated by a dotted arrow.

DOI: 10.4324/9781003183655-4

42 Two Nineteenth-Century Examples of Hexatonic-Diatonic Tonal Function

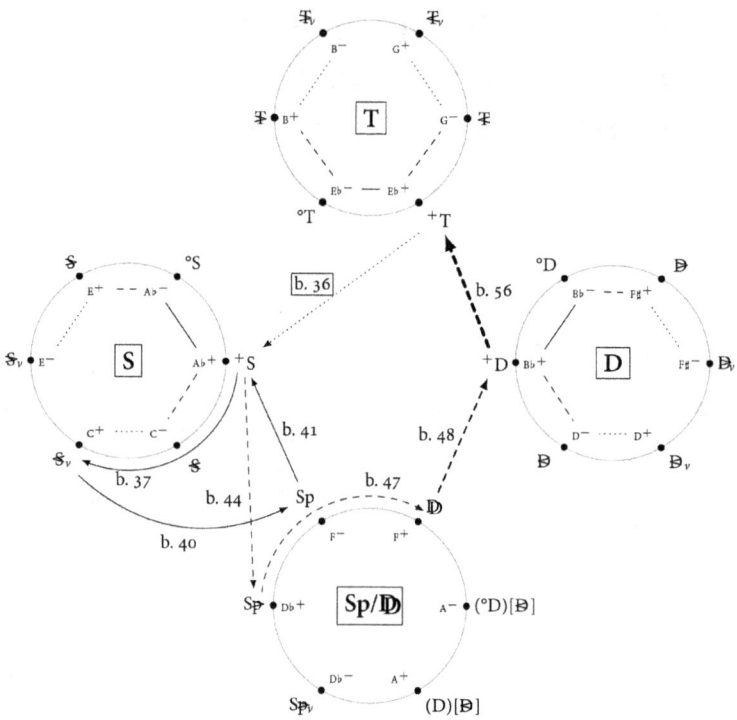

Figure 3.1 Beethoven, Piano Sonata in C minor, Op. 10, No. 1, bb. 31–55.

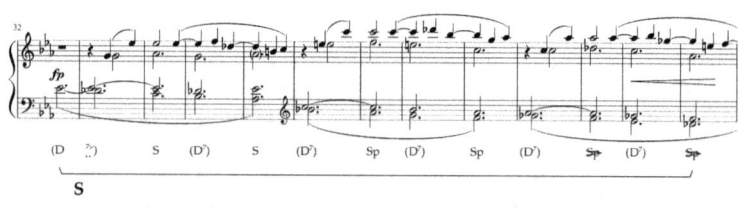

Example 3.1 Beethoven, Piano Sonata in C minor, Op. 10, No. 1, bb. 32–56, with harmonic analysis.

The subdominant function then makes two separate motions in the direction of the dominant over the course of eleven bars which explore a range of chromatically altered subdominant functions. The first motion, indicated by solid lines in Figure 3.1 (encompassing bb. 37–40), is initiated by a sudden chromatic shift to $\mathbf{S}_v$ at b. 37 and uses the dark side of the subdominant moon as a launchpad for a perfect cadence onto the subdominant parallel, °F, at b. 40. The subdominant is regained by a simple parallel transformation at b. 41, and the second motion, in the direction of the dominant and ultimately through it to the tonic, now picks up. This motion from bb. 41–56 is indicated by dashed lines. This time, in a way that is typical for a cadential progression that increasingly gains diatonic focus, the motion is slightly less dark-side than before. Thus, the motion from S to Sp at b. 44 is simply to the *Leittonwechsel* of the subdominant parallel, from where it is only two chromatic steps around the face of the Sp/$\mathbb{D}$ moon to the dominant of the dominant, from where two strong descending fifth motions, indicated by increasingly thick dashed lines, bring the music to the aimed-for secondary tonic, E♭⁺.

Riemann's own analysis of these bars, part of his three-volume study of Beethoven's piano sonatas, takes different decisions about how to label the subdominant functions.[1] What we read as motions onto S and Sp in bb. 32–40, Riemann interprets as motions onto °Sp and °S, which are the functions of the respective chords, A♭⁺ and °F, in the movement's global tonic, °C. In a similar way, while we read D♭⁺ as Sp/E♭⁺, Riemann continues to read it in the global tonic: i.e. as $\mathbf{S}$. Our notations enter alignment at b. 45, which begins the dominant lock presaging the arrival of the new tonic at b. 56. Despite the differences here, both Riemann and ourselves find the passage in question to be one exploring subdominant functions, albeit in different keys (°C for him, E♭⁺ for us). The difference is that Riemann's decision to conceive of the first part of TR as still in °C slightly obscures its pre-dominant function in the new key. (In fact, we would say that bb. 32–44 are *both* in °C and in E♭⁺: that flickering between functional states is, of course, precisely the role that a transition must enact.) This minimal difference points to an important modification of Riemann's method that we follow through in ours. While Riemann is in general, as here, content to view passages of dominant lock as what we are calling a *dominant field* (though the term is not one he uses), and extends the same logic to what we call *tonic fields* (which are, of course, simply the 'normal' notations Riemann employs in any tonal analysis where the music is in the tonic), we think it appropriate to do the same for *subdominant fields* in cases where to do so can clarify which way the music is 'facing', whether 'backwards' towards an established tonic or (as here) forwards towards a new tonic whose tonicisation is facilitated by the subdominant field.

Substituting a thematic for a harmonic logic for a moment, one can see that since bb. 32–44 begin a TR zone in a Type 3 sonata (to employ the terms used by Sonata Theory),[2] they are best viewed as the first module in a unified process that culminates in the arrival of the S zone at b. 56. A medial caesura at b. 48 is followed by eight bars of caesura fill. As the first part of a coherent transitional unit, then, bb. 32–44 might fairly be assumed to constitute a field of harmonic activity, specifically a pre-dominant one; and since the three principal chords, each prefaced twice by their own dominants, are closely related subdominant functions – S, Sp, and the *Leittonwechsel* of the second chord, S̷p – it would appear wholly uncontroversial to interpret the bars in question as a single subdominant field, represented in Example 3.1 by a bracket below the system (with the same notation repeated for the dominant and tonic fields that follow). In this first example, the subdominant field has a relatively transparent function, even given the mildly hexatonic coloration of the S̷p, and the assertion that all three fields here (**S-D-T**: note the boldface) operate as functional fields should be clear enough: this music certainly should not seem 'unresponsive to [diatonic] attentions' of the sort we are proposing.[3] What subsequent analyses will show is that, in essence, the most advanced late tonality does little to distort the operation of these fields; it merely explores slightly more dark-side harmonies, often at greater length. But while the harmony in such cases might be more complex than in this Beethoven example, the family resemblance is so strong that it seems false to deny it.

We shall substantiate that argument later. Returning now to Op. 10, No. 1, another feature of this transition progression is its orderliness. Although it apparently traverses four third-related keys (Ab^+, $°F$, Db^+, Bb^+) enroute to the new tonic, instead of dotting arbitrarily between tonic, subdominant, and dominant functions, the trajectory is tidily anticlockwise around the moons, **T**→**S**→**Sp/D̷**→**D**→**T**. Each of the *entrepôt* keys, which has its own swift V_4^6-I^6 resolution to open it up, has a subdominant function, and the entire stretch from bb. 32–46 is thus a single subdominant *field* in the key of the S zone, Eb^+. The dominant field (**D**), activated at b. 47, contains the Eb^+ functions **D̷** and **D**. The Eb^+ tonic field (**T**), which will govern the remaining sixty bars of the exposition, enters at b. 56. Thus, the entire post-primary-theme part of the exposition, from b. 32 onwards, unfolds a bilateral full close, **T⁺-S⁺-D⁺-T⁺**, by means of tonal fields that are agglomerations of the tonal functions they comprise. That is to say, each function is expanded from a single chord into an entire field of activity, with the dallying in the subdominant orbits providing, as all such delaying does, a sharpened tonal desire; the listener anticipates with rising eagerness the arrival of a definitive full close, and the use of $D^{9>}$, with its chromatic {A♮} and {G♭}, augments the pleasure of imminent arrival. Although this passage touches on the dark side, this is so only because it is a modulating passage where the whole progression is comprehensible as a single cadential passage.[4] In what is often taken to be characteristic of Beethoven's confident onward motion, this brief example represents a kind of 'optimally diatonic' use of chromaticism: the dark-side subdominant colours do not ultimately obscure a sharply drawn **S-D-T** motion.

Brahms, Concerto for Violin and Cello, Op. 102

With a composer such as Brahms the progress towards cadences can take very different routes. Cohn offers bb. 268–79 of the Double Concerto as his first prototype of a hexatonic cycle.[5] A score of bb. 264–90 is given, with harmonic analysis, as Example 3.2.

Two Nineteenth-Century Examples of Hexatonic-Diatonic Tonal Function 45

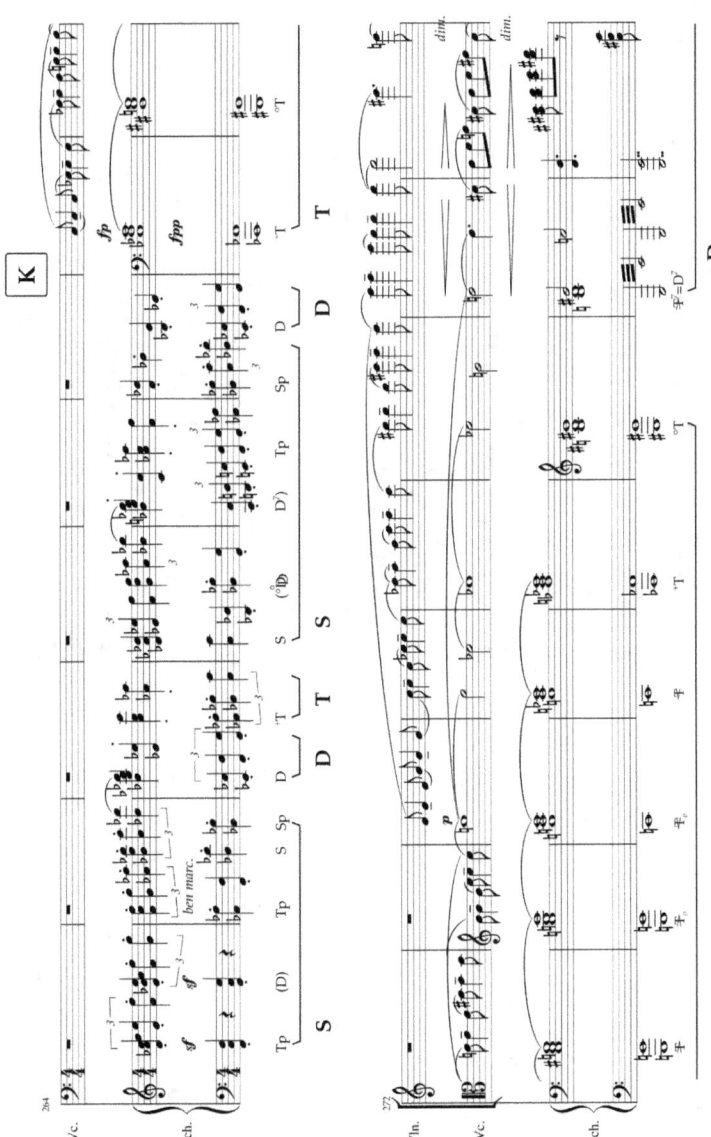

Example 3.2a. Brahms, Concerto for Violin and Cello in A minor, Op. 102, bb. 264–90, with harmonic analysis.

46 *Two Nineteenth-Century Examples of Hexatonic-Diatonic Tonal Function*

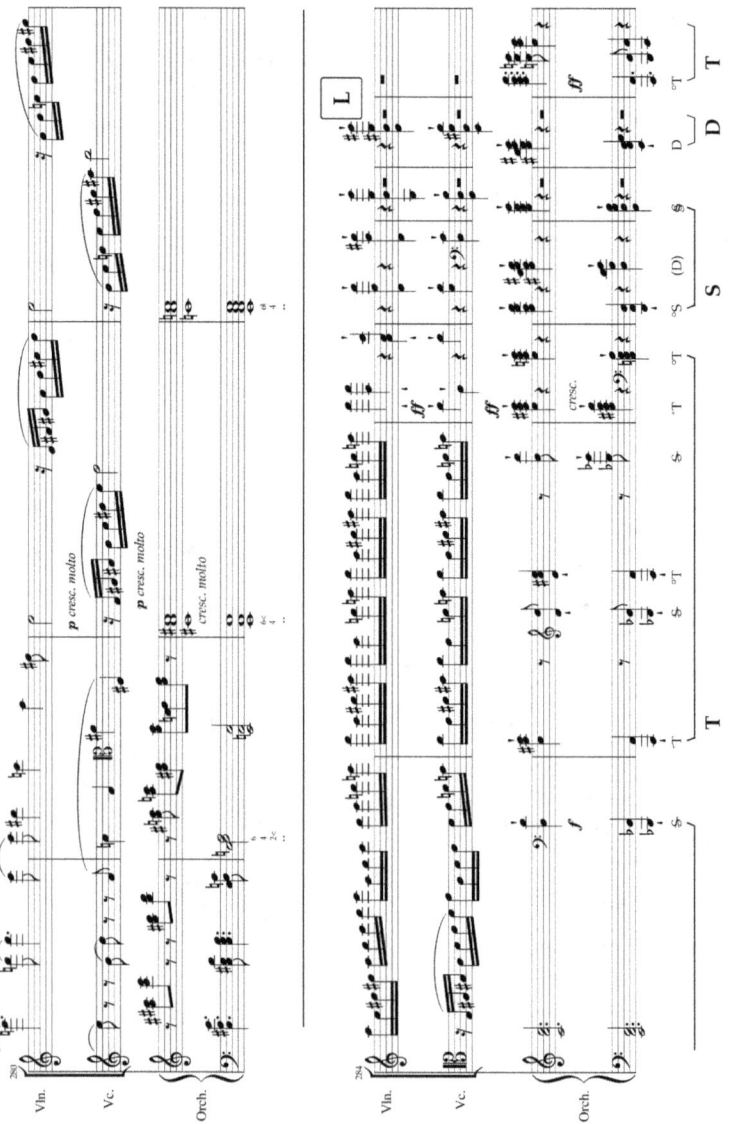

Example 3.2b. Brahms, Concerto for Violin and Cello in A minor, Op. 102, bb. 264–90, with harmonic analysis.

Two Nineteenth-Century Examples of Hexatonic-Diatonic Tonal Function

There are, Cohn notes, three properties of this passage which bear powerfully on his hexatonic theory[6]:

1. The harmonies form a 'cycle'
2. The passage has 'set-class consistency' (i.e. each chord is a triad, and therefore a member of Forte's set class 3-11)
3. Every transition between chords is 'maximally smooth', which is to say that each requires only a single semitone change

He does not name a further three properties, but they are at least as significant, musically, as the ones he chooses to mention:

4. They are the twelve bars which effect a motion from the key of $A\flat^+$, the last of the development's tonal staging posts, into the dominant of $°A$, the movement's tonic
5. They are, by definition, developmental in character
6. They come at the end of the development's retransition, in which conspicuous raising of energy levels at b. 250, and again at b. 262, have already given conventional indications of approaching recapitulation

The drop in dynamic level to *pianissimo* at b. 270, with a D-T cadence that establishes a pseudo-individualised local $A\flat^+$, delays the point of recapitulation by knocking the wind out of the preceding music, while the hexatonic colouring to which Cohn directs his attention enables Brahms to reach the tonic as if by the back door, half-unnoticed, at b. 284, before being reinforced through a gesturally obvious cadence in b. 290.

Figure 3.2 graphs the harmonic motions of the passage that Cohn analyses, and it includes important harmonic motions before and after. Cohn's selected bars begin at the top of the diagram, on $C^{+7} - 3^{+7}$ of the local tonic in this passage, $A\flat^+ -$ a chord that is here functioning locally as D^7 of the Tp to which it closes half way through the bar (see the fifth bar of Example 3.2). We hear $A\flat^+$ as the local tonic here because it has been firmly established by the immediately preceding context, and bb. 264–70 exhibit a functionally straightforward pair of bilateral full closes by means of a sequence of six functional fields: **S-D-T-S-D-T**. (Again, boldface is used to distinguish fields from local functions.) Figure 3.2 opens with the second of those bilateral full closes, (D)Tp-Sp-D-T, which is indicated by increasingly thick dashed lines in the graph. In the broader context of this movement, the purpose of the hexatonic cycling which now begins (and is illustrated by dotted lines) is to break the tonal hold of $A\flat^+$ and to re-establish, as if by a process of chromatic magic, the movement's tonic, $°A$.

A simple motion treating $A\flat^+$ as $\text{\textcurrency}_y/°A$ could have enabled Brahms to effect a fairly swift cadence: $\text{\textcurrency}_y$-D-$°T$, i.e. $A\flat^+$-E^+-$°A$ (where the motion from $\text{\textcurrency}_y$ to D would require a change of only two semitones, two steps clockwise around the dominant moon). But instead, Brahms offers a kind of late-tonal equivalent of the traditional circle of fifths, in this case a hexatonic cycling that is indicated by the

48 Two Nineteenth-Century Examples of Hexatonic-Diatonic Tonal Function

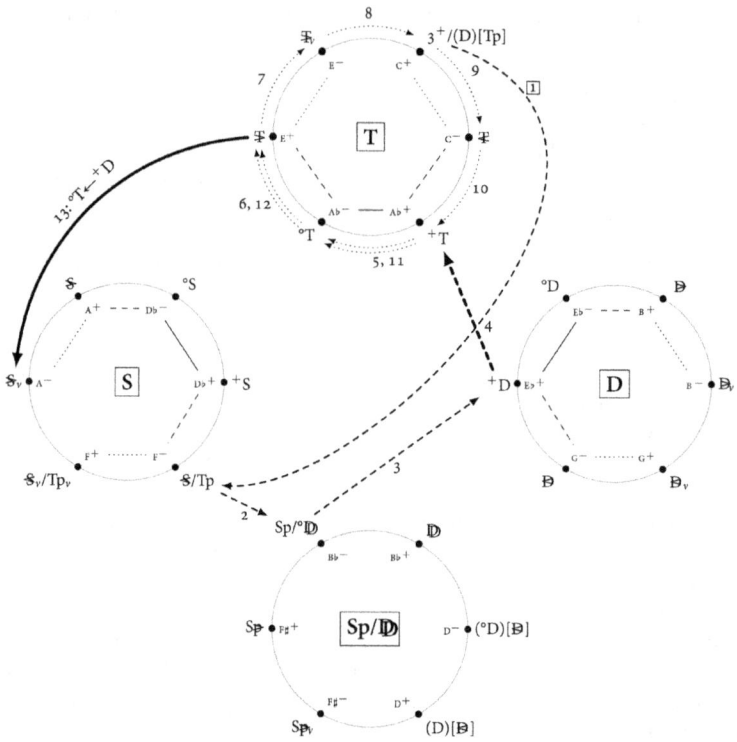

Figure 3.2 Brahms, Concerto for Violin and Cello, Op. 102, first movement, bb. 268–90, tonal function (viewed in A♭).

lines orbiting one-and-a-third times around the tonic moon (the motions are labelled 5–12, and shown by dotted lines). Although D/°A is touched on in b. 272, the chord is clearly the third node of a clockwise hexatonic motion, T⁺-°T-𝔅. It is heard as part of a tonic passage, and its function is properly analysed as a tonic *Leittonwechsel*: i.e. it is not (yet) D/°A. The moment at which the function shifts, almost imperceptibly but still clearly, is b. 278, where the rising arpeggios in the solo instruments, which had been uninterrupted throughout the hexatonic passage of bb. 270–77, are replaced by a descent in the violin and a new four-note rising motive played antiphonally between solo cello and woodwind. In this bar, a chord that on its first appearance had a murky tonic function is now transformed into a dominant.

Several gestures guarantee that the listener will not miss the moment of conversion: (1) the change in motive; (2) the addition of a seventh to the harmony; and (3) the new texture, with the woodwind joining the string sonority heard till now, and – most unmistakably – an expectant timpani roll on the dominant root, {E}. From the perspective of a hexatonic view of the music, there is nothing really

Two Nineteenth-Century Examples of Hexatonic-Diatonic Tonal Function 49

significant about this bar: it is simply the eighth hexatonic motion around the tonic moon. But from a Riemannian functional perspective, this final motion is crucial. The timpani's four-bar roll on the dominant is held as a pedal for six bars by the low strings. Now having revealed itself, by the simple expedient of occupying the musical ground for so long, as a putative dominant, the function is further confirmed by the following six bars, which end the development with an insistent, and metrically quickening, progression: dotted notes halve their length from minim to crotchet in the space of two bars, before settling in a steady crotchet tread with antiphonal exchanges between the orchestra and paired soloists in bb. 286–9. The harmonic progression cements the dominant function as it unfolds another bilateral cadence, this time back into the movement's overall tonic: °T-°S-(D)-𝔻-D-°T.

To show this passage from the perspective of its cadential target, Figure 3.3 reads these same harmonic motions from the perspective of the global

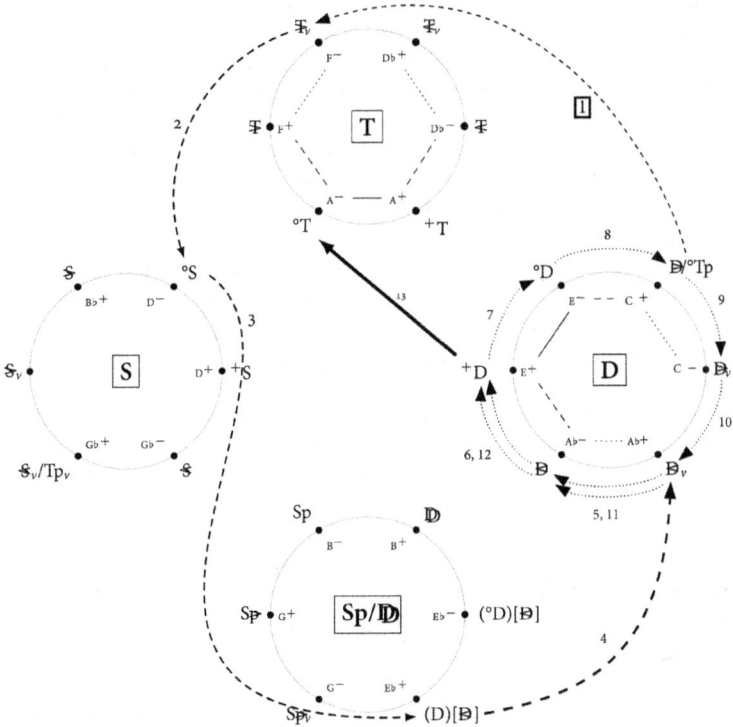

Figure 3.3 Brahms, Concerto for Violin and Cello, Op. 102, i, bb. 268–90, tonal function (viewed in °A).

tonic. The first diagram is turned through ninety degrees clockwise, and each moon is realigned so that its tonic and dominant functions face 'inwards'. Now, the first four moves of this passage, which swirl round the dark side of the tonic moon before vaulting to the mixed moon, and thence the dark-side dominant harmony of ⊠$_v$, indicate the tonal vagrancy of these bars from the perspective of the global tonic. Although on some level a Schenkerian reading would theoretically insist on a listener's ability to hear the A♭$^+$ passage as a prolongation of the dominant via a tonicisation of its major third, we do not think that any listener could really be imagined to *hear* this music as directly prolonging the tonic: it is, after all, a different thing to *understand* that something is the case and to *hear* it as such. The wildness of the lunar motion here shows the sensitivity of this graphing system to what is functionally heard: retrospectively, we might understand that the progression in A♭$^+$ was functionally prolonging °A, but only in a highly chromatic way. In general, motions that pass between the open faces of the moons, rather than (as in Figure 3.3) darting from one dark side to another, will tend to create a sense of groundedness, however brief, in the tonality whose 'planet' they orbit. This is the case with the first four motions of Figure 3.2, where, as we have just shown, the relative clarity of the passage between moons S and D reflects the strength of the tonal projection of A♭$^+$ at this point. But moves 5–12 simply circle hexatonically around a moon that reveals itself to be the °A dominant moon, as what retrospectively emerges, from the recapitulatory perspective, as the pseudo-individuated 'tonic', A♭$^+$, imperceptibly gives way to the real dominant of which it was always only a chromatic alteration (⊠$_v$).

There is no doubt that a focus on the hexatonic motion in the closing bars of the development reveals something about how Brahms moves, harmony to harmony. The motions between chords are not in any direct way diatonic, and the hexatonic logic explains the progression better, at least at first. But the progressions are nevertheless *indirectly* diatonic insofar as these hexatonic motions allow two processes to occur simultaneously: first, a hexatonic cycle (tonicised by the 'old' dominant, i.e. (D)A♭$^+$) gradually dissolves the sense of the old tonal centre at the same time as transforming A♭ into the 'new' dominant, D/°A, which precipitates the recapitulation. In other words, by a different means Brahms is performing the same modulation-plus-cadence process of Beethoven's Op. 10, No. 1 Piano Sonata, by converting a function from one key into a function in another (in Beethoven's case, the conversion was from a subdominant field in °C, the focus of Riemann's analysis, into a subdominant field in E♭$^+$, the focus of ours). And as can be seen in Figure 3.3 – the diagrammatic representation of the motion into the target key, °A – Brahms's retransition traces the same Classical anticlockwise lunar motion, **T**→**S**→**Sp**→/**D**→**D**→**T**, as Beethoven. The motion begins, in fact, *before* the cadence into A♭$^+$ that opens the passage: the stopping points on the **T** (i.e. ℞$_v$), **S** (i.e. °S), **Sp/D** (i.e. (D)[⊠]), and **D** (i.e. ⊠$_v$) moons are, as we

Two Nineteenth-Century Examples of Hexatonic-Diatonic Tonal Function 51

have indicated, remote functions indeed in the target °A, and yet even these chords – locally a much more lucid (D)Tp-Sp-D-T in A♭⁺ – are retrospectively tugged into a legible, if dark-side, functional trajectory. The power of tonality to force any progression at all into an ultimately legible tonicising configuration is breath-taking.

As the elephantine curves and the complex functional notations (°D-P̌ᵥ -°S-(D)[D̂]) for the first four motions show, Brahms's route back to his tonic is highly chromatic. But the orbit of the dominant moon in the passage that Cohn analyses extracts a second potent effect from the dissolution of a tonal centre we have just mentioned: by dissolving a remote relation to the target key, Brahms is able to permit the wished-for dominant to emerge with maximum clarity – in concert with the extremely vigorous gestures of the orchestra and soloists – for the recapitulation-launching perfect cadence. Brahms's harmonic motions here chart a stimulating course from A♭⁺ to °A, but there is no Copernican revolution between Beethoven's style and Brahms's: a 'second' kind of tonal thinking does not enter into play. In both pieces, the geocentric orbit around Planet Tonality remains in place. The orbits are slightly more eccentric, but they are recognisably of the same sort.

Once more, a contrast between a Schenkerian and our Riemannian perspective points to an important step in the direction of a new functional theory of late tonal music. A Schenkerian analysis such as that shown in Figure 3.4 would make the power of the global tonic apparent by different means. (Unlike Figures 3.2 and 3.3, this graph includes the first chord of b. 268 in order to show the consonant preparation of the melodic {B♭}.) The chords leading up to the cadence in A♭⁺ would, from the perspective of the global tonic, be shown to be subordinate to the prolongation of the upper third of the dominant: in other words, their function would be judged diatonic, at a lower structural level than that of the *Ursatz* that is resumed after the interruption, at the start of the recapitulation. A Schenkerian reading would thus 'diatonicise' what appears (from the global perspective) as chromaticism here, by reading it as a series of diatonic functions within a non-tonic *Stufe*. By contrast,

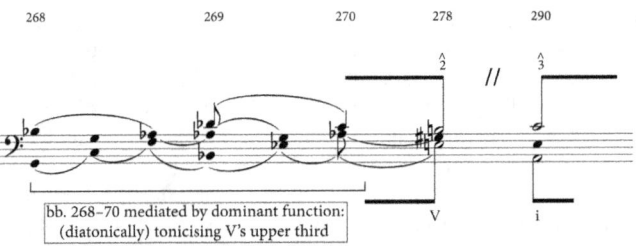

Figure 3.4 Schenkerian analysis of bb. 268–90.

a Riemannian approach can have its cake and eat it: the progression can be shown to have both a diatonic identity within $A\flat^+$ and also a chromatic – but still functional – identity within $°A$. From the perspective of the entire movement, the functional relation between any given chord and the global tonic is, from a Schenkerian perspective, (a) always to be understood diatonically, and (b) insofar as it has a chromatic relation to the global tonic, that function is mediated by the local *Stufe* and 'diatonicised'. But from the Riemannian perspective we are proposing here, the functional relation is direct and unmediated, and chromaticism is not forced into a diatonic bottle: remote tonal functions do not require the 'special pleading' of a *Stufe*-level diatonic pillar to maintain a strong function. (For more on this idea, see Chapter 5.)

It is worth pausing to consider the implications of this difference when tonality is taken as an analysis of its society. One of Adorno's central arguments about tonal music is that it contains the sediment of the history out of which it emerges. Art and social experience are not mere analogues: there is a 'metalogical' connection between them.[7] The result of this connection is the ultimately impossible process of music's 'dialectic of spiritualization', in which the more that art strives to achieve autonomy from society, the more merely empirical it becomes, the less autonomous and the less in any sense a 'work' that is separate from society.[8] In the dialectic of spiritualisation, the musical work aims for mastery over its internal operations of form and content. This mastery, or 'domination' as Adorno also calls it, is domination within the artwork with the purpose of affording a critique of the domination that lies at the heart of bourgeois society. Tonality has the form it has because modern society has the form it has, and tonal music has the implicit potential to bend the form of tonality to the critique of that society. Both that society and its music are grounded in Enlightenment rationality, and both follow its totalising logic, in which rationality itself becomes ideological, or as Adorno and Horkheimer put it in the Preface to *Dialectic of Enlightenment*, 'enlightenment reverts to mythology'.[9]

Putting this metalogical relation of music and society in the terms of the 'triumvirs' of tonality with which we began the book, the Riemannian approach shows how the central triumviral power exerts direct, unmediated control over the chordal particular, without the need of any kind of intermediary. This enables the local incident to 'feel' to some extent free from central tonal control, and yet all of the time to be subjected directly to that control. On a Schenkerian view, by contrast, the local incident will always 'feel' circumscribed to the confines of a particular local tonicisation, and will therefore not 'feel' free from tonal control at all. The local tonic acts as the local commander, holding order in place on behalf of the distant, central triumvirate. Schenker's view of tonality is thus a metaphorically weak one: if every harmony must submit to a local tonicising force (the local commander called the *Stufe*) that, in turn, is submitted to the global tonal centre, then the system is being held in place by individual elements that 'know' themselves to be subordinated by a complex machinery to a central tonal aim. In such circumstances an individual in a totally rationalised world might not strive to resist or even critique the totality. All resistance would appear to be futile, because every motion that is transacted in the local space will simply be submitted to the global function as a guarantor of the tonal hegemony. That might make the model of society articulated by music that is understood in Schenkerian terms seem, from the perspective of a putative critic of the society, passive to the point of being willingly submissive to domination. But the social quality of chromatic music when it is viewed from a Riemannian perspective is perhaps even more horrifying. In the absence of any sense that it must submit to a local authority acting on behalf of the totalitarian centre, the individual feels itself 'more free', unbounded by the need to submit to the global hegemony. Without the mediating *Stufe*, such an individual might feel that there is nothing to translate the free chromatic agent to the diatonic will of the tonal hegemon, and therefore motion at the local level can, even if only temporarily, as a kind of chromatic carnival, exercise genuine freedom. The Riemannian perspective, though, shows that this vision of local, carnivalesque freedom is illusory. That which feels itself separate and free from society is in fact 'pseudo-individualised'.[10] 'Free' tonality is shown not to have effected a Copernican revolution – and yet, paradoxically, in so doing it reveals all the more clearly what would be necessary for such a revolution to take place.

In a technical-musical sense, the different analyses of the social structures that are metalogically represented in the musical work hinge on the small but crucial difference between the implications of Schenker's and Riemann's understandings of tonicisation. Riemann's approximate equivalent of the Schenkerian *Stufe* is his idea of 'intermediate cadences', and from the perspective of the global tonic in the Brahms Double Concerto, the opening $A\flat^+$ passage is an example. That is, it is one of a number of cases whose keys, Riemann says (in a passage we have already quoted) should 'be considered as tonics, without, however, their tonal functions being altered'.[11] Within the $°A$ sonata, the 'true' function of this entire $A\flat^+$ section is dialectically a dominant one, specifically $\mathfrak{D}_v$; and that function is not altered by the fact that, within its immediate context, $A\flat^+$ should be considered as Tonic. Viewed as an intermediate full close in $A\flat^+$, the progression in bb. 268–70, followed by the full close back into the tonic in bb. 278–90, would therefore be written as:

((D)Tp-Sp-D)$\mathfrak{D}_v$-D-T

The point of transition from a tonal centring on $A\flat^+$ to one on $°A$ is here captured tidily by the motion '$\mathfrak{D}_v$-D', a shorthand notation for the fact that a hexatonic motion enables an intermediate cadence in the first key to be harnessed functionally as the preparation for the dominant in the second key. The Schenkerian logic of the *Stufe*, as shown in Figure 3.4, also holds that such a key has a global and a local function, but with the difference that unless the global function is already diatonic – i.e. is chord II, IV, V, etc.

– its global function will be understood to be mediated by a diatonic *Stufe*. In this case, then, A♭⁺ is mediated by V, and has some kind of dominant function; on the Riemannian view the function is also a dominant one, but is now specifically labelled 𝒟ᵥ and has a distance from the dominant function that can be precisely mapped. This difference between the Schenkerian and Riemannian perspectives is not especially important for music such as this, but it becomes important in more complex situations, which is why it is instructive to lay out the theoretical distinction clearly now, where it is easier to see. In the case of a passage like this one from the Brahms Double Concerto, there is no need to invoke the idea that we are presenting as unmediated access between the global tonic and every other chord, because the passage clearly opens on A♭⁺ and moves to °A, and consequently it would make sense in most cases to read the motions of bb. 270–90 in terms of a modulation from diatonic function in A♭⁺ to diatonic function in °A. But in music where the freedom of tonality is greater, the absence of mediation between diatonic background and (sometimes extremely) chromatic functions at the foreground, and the obviation of the need to 'diatonicise' chromaticism within a single functional progression, becomes an important part of the analytical method, as will be seen in the following Chapters. In such music there is often no option of choosing to view a chord of A♭⁺ in an °A context as if it were tonicising the upper third of the dominant, for the very good reason that no dominant is present. Such music would pose immense problems for a Schenkerian theory of prolongation, where complex chromatic functions generally require such a diatonic mediation in the middle ground. But in such a case, the Riemannian 𝒟ᵥ function would always remain possible, and suddenly the possibility that even the most chromatic music can have a strong functional identity – a possibility that has been underdeveloped for many decades – emerges as an entirely realistic truth that can be grasped.

Notes

1 Hugo Riemann, *L. van Beethovens sämtliche Klavier-Solosonaten. Äesthetische und formal-technische Analyse mit historischen Notizen*, vol. 1: Sonate (Leipzig: Max Hesses Verlag, 1918), 280–1.
2 James A. Hepokoski and Warren Darcy, *Elements of Sonata Theory: Norms, Types, and Deformations in the Late Eighteenth-Century Sonata* (Oxford: Oxford University Press, 2006).
3 Richard Cohn, 'Introduction to Neo-Riemannian Theory: A Survey and a Historical Perspective', *Journal of Music Theory* 42, no. 2 (1998): 167–80, 168.
4 Within a non-modulating primary or secondary theme, however, such a harmony as C⁺ in an E♭⁺ context would be unusual until later in the century.
5 Richard Cohn, 'Maximally Smooth Cycles, Hexatonic Systems, and the Analysis of Late-Romantic Triadic Progressions', *Music Analysis* 15, no. 1 (1996): 9–40, 13–17.

6 Ibid., 15.
7 Theodor W. Adorno, *Negative Dialectics*, ed. and trans. E. B. Ashton (London: Routledge, 1973), 135–6.
8 Theodor W. Adorno, *Aesthetic Theory*, ed. Gretel Adorno and Rolf Tiedermann, trans. Robert Hullot-Kentor (Minneapolis: University of Minnesota Press, 1997), 91–3.
9 Max Horkheimer and Theodor W. Adorno, *Dialectic of Enlightenment: Philosophical Fragments*, ed. Gunzelin Schmid Noerr, trans. Edmund Jephcott (Stanford: Stanford University Press, 2002), xviii.
10 Ibid., 125.
11 Hugo Riemann, *Harmony Simplified*, 128.

Bibliography

Adorno, Theodor W. *Negative Dialectics*, edited by and translated by E.B. Ashton. London: Routledge, 1973.

———. *Aesthetic Theory*, edited by Gretel Adorno, and Rolf Tiedermann, translated by Robert Hullot-Kentor, 91–3. Minneapolis: University of Minnesota Press, 1997.

Caplin, William. *Classical Form: A Theory of Formal Functions for the Instrumental Music of Haydn, Mozart, and Beethoven*. Oxford: Oxford University Press, 1998.

Cohn, Richard. 'Maximally Smooth Cycles, Hexatonic Systems, and the Analysis of Late-Romantic Triadic Progressions', *Music Analysis* 15, no. 1 (1996): 9–40.

———. 'Introduction to Neo-Riemannian Theory: A Survey and a Historical Perspective', *Journal of Music Theory* 42, no. 2 (1998): 167–80.

Hepokoski, James A., and Warren Darcy. *Elements of Sonata Theory: Norms, Types, and Deformations in the Late Eighteenth-century Sonata*. Oxford: Oxford University Press, 2006.

Horkheimer, Max, and Theodor W. Adorno. *Dialectic of Enlightenment: Philosophical Fragments*, edited by Gunzelin Schmid Noerr, translated by Edmund Jephcott. Stanford: Stanford University Press, 2002.

Riemann, Hugo. *Harmony Simplified; or, the Theory of the Tonal Functions of Chords*. London: Augener, 1893 [1896].

———. *L. van Beethovens sämtliche Klavier-Solosonaten. Äesthetische und formaltechnische Analyse mit historischen Notizen* vol. 1: Sonate. Leipzig: Max Hesses Verlag, 1918.

4 The Multiple Lives of Seventh Chords

In this chapter, we consider one of the most common criticisms levelled at Riemann's system of harmonic labelling: namely, its hypothetical reduction of all extended sonorities to triads. Two principal problems are associated with this approach: (1) The stylistic importance of smooth voice leading to late tonal music is consequently downplayed; and (2) The paradoxical enharmonic effects of certain seventh-chord progressions disappear if they are so reduced. Richard Cohn has explored these problems in depth and we summarise the arguments for a unique tetrachordal syntax in his book *Audacious Euphony*, before considering some of the problems (alongside the many benefits) that emerge if they are accepted. Building on this, we look to maintain the graphical elegance of NRT – the ways in which it can capture the totality of smooth voice-leading relations visually – but to reinvest its representations of pitch space with functional energy. This leads us to a new model: our 'octatonic-submoon' function graph. We use this to generate a novel reading of Chopin's Op. 28, No. 4, in which dominant- and half-diminished seventh chords that belong to the same octatonic scale are interpreted as having the same function (albeit to varying extents); these octatonic scales, and the chords that belong to them, are conceptualised as submoons that orbit the triadic functional moons theorised in Chapters 2 and 3. We then analyse another passage from Waltraute's Plaint (Act 1, Scene 3, bb. 1296–310) in which movement between seventh chords is *not* smooth, nor conventionally functional. We argue that this example can help to demonstrate a hidden kinship between Riemannian and neo-Riemannian systems, however: when reduced to triads, the sevenths in question might have a number of functional designations; the position of the relevant tetrachord on the octatonic-submoon diagram verifies the functional multivalence disclosed by the original Riemannian labelling – i.e. it might be positioned at the boundary between two functions – but it can also determine which of these functions is ultimately stronger, on the basis of which submoon to which it actually belongs.

Once More on Rhetorical Dialectics

> [N]either a mere play of counterpoint, nor the most fantastic art of figuration and most inventive harmonising, either could or should

DOI: 10.4324/9781003183655-5

The Multiple Lives of Seventh Chords 57

transform a theme so characteristically, and present it with such manifold and changed expression – yet leaving it always recognisable – as true dramatic art can do quite naturally. Hardly anything could afford a plainer proof of this, than a pursuit of that simple song of the "Rhein-daughters" through all the changing passions of the four-part drama down to Hagen's Watch-song in the first act of *Götterdämmerung*, where it certainly takes on a form which – to me at least – makes it inconceivable as the theme of a symphonic movement, albeit it is still governed by the laws of harmony and thematicism, though purely in their application to the drama. To attempt to apply the results of such a method to the symphony, however, must lead to the latter's ruin; for here would appear as a far-fetched Effect what follows there from well-found motives.

– Richard Wagner, 'On the Application of Music to the Drama' (1879)[1]

As this quotation makes clear, there is something about the Hagen Chords from Act 1, Scene 2 of *Götterdämmerung* that defies traditional (i.e. symphonic) musical logic (see Example 4.1a). On the one hand, they clearly reference the decidedly functional bø^7-C major progression from Act 1, Scene i of *Das Rheingold* (see Example 4.1b): the Rheinmaidens' expression of their joy in the gold.[2] This is not only a matter of extra-musical association: Hagen's progression is the only transformation from a closely voiced Ø^7 to a V^7 (as opposed to a triad) that features the inward-pointing contrary motion of the 'Joy' motif's characteristic outer-voice wedge shape. Contrapuntal behaviour – characteristic of resolving augmented-sixth or leading-tone seventh chords – closely associates this leitmotif with tonal behaviour, even if there is no imminent sign of a return to a diatonic context.[3] On the other hand, this progression is enharmonically paradoxical: irrespective of the counterpoint, how can it be associated with tonal behaviour if it cannot be reconciled with a single key? That it *is* paradoxical might not be immediately apparent; the Generalised Intervallic Structure (GIS), shown below, attempts to make this idea clear, drawing the reader's attention to the contradiction between two apperceptions (see Figure 4.1).[4]

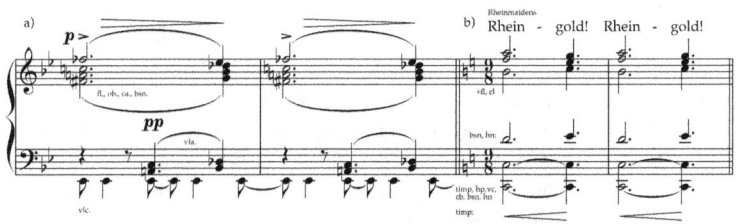

Example 4.1. (a) The 'Hagen chords', *Götterdämmerung*, Act 1, Scene 2, bb. 878–9; *(b)* The 'Joy in the Gold' motif, *Das Rheingold*, Scene 1, bb. 540–1.

58 The Multiple Lives of Seventh Chords

a♭	$\hat{1}$	$\hat{2}$	$\hat{3}$	$\hat{4}$	$\hat{5}$	$\hat{6}$	$\hat{7}$
7							g
6					f♯		
5							
4					e♮	f♭	
3					e♭		
2							
1				d♭			
0			c				
e							
t		b♭					
9	a♮						
8							

♯6, ♯1, 3, ♭6   correct resolutions;
f♯, a, c, f♭,   <u>not</u> a 'seventh chord'

♯6, ♯1, 3, ♯5   incorrect res.;
f♯, a, c, e♮,   <u>is</u> a seventh chord

Figure 4.1 A tonal GIS (generalised intervallic structure) modelling the possible resolutions of f♯ø⁷ to E♭7. The gamut of chromatic pitch classes is represented on the *y* axis; diatonic scale-degrees in A♭ are listed on the *x* axis.

Apperception 1: The first chord of the Hagen progression is *composed of four different scale degrees* (as are all seventh chords more generally).

Apperception 2: If we hear the original 'Rheingold!' motif behind Hagen's corrupted repetition – an essential step if we are properly to understand the new leitmotif's role in the drama – then each of the implied scale degrees in the first chord should *resolve to a different scale degree* in the second chord.

If the latter apperception is accepted, pc 4 must be heard as ♭$\hat{6}$, so that it might discharge to $\hat{5}$ (note that Wagner in fact spells this as F♭), and pc 6 must be heard as ♯$\hat{6}$, so that it may rise to $\hat{7}$ (again, note that Wagner does in fact spell this as F♯). The resultant scale degree confederation ♯$\hat{6}$, ♯$\hat{1}$, $\hat{3}$, and ♭$\hat{6}$, however, *cannot be heard to manifest a seventh chord*; there is no seventh (i.e. $\hat{5}$). But a listener will not be persuaded of this: if they hear the f♯ø⁷ chord in isolation, *it will necessarily be heard as a seventh* (Apperception 1).

Imagine an alternative hearing, then: f♯ø⁷ forms a ♯6̂-♯1̂-3̂-♯5̂ alliance in A♭ (note the four different scale-step designations).⁵ The problem with this latter reading is that one would hear the movement from pitch classes <4,3> as 'prolonging' the same scale degree (i.e. ♯5̂-♮5̂) rather than as discharging from one discrete scale step to another. If we want to maintain Apperception (1) and Apperception (2) – both reasonable in isolation but impossible in combination – then a subtle paradox emerges, which the GIS brings into vivid relief. It is this paradox, we argue, that makes this progression 'far-fetched' from a symphonic point of view (*thus spake* Wagner), but ideal for representing musically a dramatically motivated development (i.e. the perversion of the Gold's purity by Hagen's avarice).

Surely this last example exposes a blind spot within the field of vision of Riemann's harmonic theory? His routine assumption that seventh chords are mere extensions of triads removes the distinctly tetrachordal paradox of Hagen's chords from view: i.e. its rhetorical-dialectical essence. While it is certainly the case that 'characteristic dissonances' might be used to distinguish S- and D-functioning chords from the Tonic, or to prevent parallels (particularly between S and D),⁶ the *Tristan*-revolution – so neo-Riemannian theory has argued – is irreducible to such traditional part-writing explanations.

Richard Cohn has observed that smooth voice leading between seventh chords, so essential to Wagner's harmonic style, becomes disjunctive if we try to interpret them, *à la* Riemann, triadically.⁷ He gives the example of gø⁷ moving to C⁷ – a transformation that requires only two units of semitonal voice-leading work – and contrasts it with the move from °B♭ to C⁺ (i.e. the triads that the sevenths would implicitly represent, according to Riemann) that would result in six. One might question the usefulness of this example: is it not simply a move from Chord ii to V in F minor, irrespective of the progression's cardinality? Cohn is not arguing against the possibility of such labels; he suggests instead that it is the smooth voice-leading relationship between chords (as opposed to their functions) that are constitutive of the Wagner style: *voice leading rather than function is generative.*

Building on the work of Bass, Boretz, Lewin, Childs, Callender, and others, Cohn argues that there is a syntax immanent in the tetrachordal universe that is in some sense distinct from a triadic one:

> Wagner famously blew open the gates to a compositional field cohabited by V⁷ and Ø⁷ chords whose interactions were disciplined *neither by tonality nor by patterned sequential repetition*. Succeeding generations of composers romped on this *Tristan* field for a half-century and more, using semitonal voice leading to connect Ø⁷ chords directly to each other, and

to V^7 chords, in a manner that *defied diatonic/tonal coherence more frequently than not.*[8]

How do seventh chords relate to one another, if not tonally? The short answer is 'through smooth voice leading'. But, as always with Cohn, the emphasis is not merely on transformations – the myriad ways in which a chord might be semitonally adjusted – but, rather, on the overall 'compositional system' that might be generalised from the agglomeration of those transformations.[9] He hypothesises that half-diminished and dominant-seventh chords function as harmonic substitutes for fully diminished sevenths. While this might seem to put 'the dissonant cart before the relatively consonant horse',[10] there is a compelling formal efficiency to Cohn's argument. The three possible fully diminished harmonies (i.e. $\{0,3,6,9\}$, $\{1,4,7,T\}$; $\{2,5,8,E\}$)[11] can be used to generate all twenty-four half-diminished and dominant sevenths by adjusting individually each of their chord tones upwards and downwards by a semitone. For example, both B^7 (B–D♯–F♯–A) and $C\varnothing^7$ (C–E♭–G♭–B♭) "minimally perturb" the same fully diminished seventh (i.e. $\{0,3,6,9\}$): the dominant tetrachord displaces its first chord tone downwards by a minor second, while the half-diminished sonority adjusts its last chord tone upwards by a semitone.

Cohn uses the 4-Cube Trio (adapted from Jack Douthett) to model the chromatic, tetrachordal pitch-space universe that results if fully diminished sevenths and smooth voice-leading connections between tetrachords are privileged in this way (see Figure 4.2). Because of the inherent symmetry of the [0369] sets around which this space is built, one can talk of neither 'up' nor 'down'; smooth voice-leading operations work their way around a delimited but ultimately decentred space.[12] What matters most, on this view, is the motion between chordal nodes, rather than the sensuous quality of the nodes themselves. To borrow Daniel Harrison's formulation, '[tetrachordal] objects lose stability as things-in-themselves and [...] are reduced solely to things-in-transformational-relations ...[; they become] an absence of sorts, an empty circle in a node-arrow graph, a thing in such constant becoming that it has no being'.[13] It is vital to point out, though, that Cohn understands this apparent suspension of harmony's 'sensuous dimension'[14] as (1) provisional – a heuristic step that might be reversed (see below); and (2) as itself being dependent on an underlying metaphor of embodiment. He argues (a) that composers *might*, but need not, 'wander' through the entirety of the chromatic space '*as if* oblivious to the semantic values of classical tonality and the syntactic obligations that they impose'; and (b) that the 4-Cube Trio provides a useful means of representing this *particular* possibility graphically.[15] (Our use of the conditional and Cohn's use of simile are intended to stress the epistemological, as opposed to ontological, nature of this claim; it should not be reified into a prescription about how one *should* hear.[16]) Cruising along a motorway in a car is a comparable sensation to navigating chromatic tetrachordal space, he (implicitly) argues.[17] In the

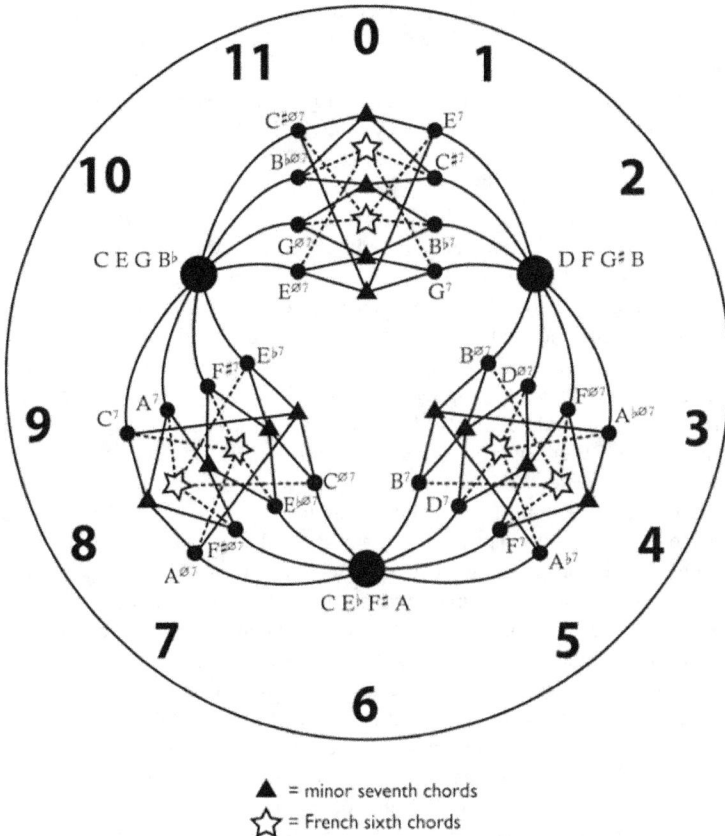

▲ = minor seventh chords
☆ = French sixth chords

Figure 4.2 Jack Douthett's 4-Cube Trio, Figure 7.16, *Audacious Euphony* (2012, 158). (NB: There is a typo: the diminished seventh at 10 o'clock should begin on C♯.) Reproduced by permission of Oxford University Press (USA).

same way that one's experience of driving is not dependent on a singular event, but rather a combination of such events – the feeling of movement and speed – one's experience of 4-Cube-Trio passages is not of individual chords, *per se*, but rather of movement across a chromatic space. (Given the slower tempos composers often use to articulate these kinds of progression, one might debate the usefulness of this motorway analogy – listeners are invited to savour each and every transformation rather than to zoom through them indiscriminately – but it still implies a form of embodied experience.)

To return to point (1), Cohn is aware of the dichotomy at the heart of Riemann's music theories: namely, the overdetermined nature of the 'function' concept, which (potentially) collapses the 'ontological difference between thinking of the dominant as a relation and thinking of it as an actual chord'.[18] So, while motions might not 'hearken to the call of the tonal forces to which those harmonies are normally subjected under the terms of classical tonality [i.e. the need of tendency tones and extensions to resolve]' – in which case the more neutral set-class label [0258] works wonders – those 'summons' *can* be heeded, if a composer so chooses: 'dissonant sonorities [can] revert to their inborn behaviours [i.e. the need to resolve rather than to proceed to another dissonance], sometimes retrospectively projecting those behaviours onto their predecessors'.[19] One might generalise, then, that there are two kinds of relation between [0258] chords: a transformational variety, that is invoked when smooth motion across a chromatic space is emphasised, and a more bodily kind, activated when 'the fraught tensions and attractions, gravities and magnetisms of tonality' are restored. In the latter circumstance, chords are valued for their own intrinsic quality – for the inner tensions they must discharge or for the sense of subsequent repose that they can create.[20]

If one takes Cohn at his word – semitonal voice-leading connections between *Tristan*-genus chords 'defy diatonic/tonal coherence more frequently than not' – then one might generalise that 4-Cube-Trio behaviours are essentially non-tonal, while disjunct and (presumably fifth-based?) progressions re-activate tonality. (Cohn is not actually explicit about those conditions that might reactivate tonal intention, as we discuss below.) An unfortunate consequence of this idea is that it is all too easy to reify Cohn's graphic system – of distinct transformational-seventh-chord and functional-triadic universes – and to erect a tonal-atonal binary off the back of it. While Cohn's mission is to assemble epistemological possibilities to enrich the listening experience, rather than to pronounce on questions of harmonic 'truth', it is difficult to ignore the fact that claiming something to be fundamentally incoherent – i.e. not logically or aesthetically integrated – is a much stronger claim than simply asking us 'to suspend some overlearned habits [of diatonic music theory]'.[21] And even the far milder claim that the 4-Cube Trio might be thought to map the smooth movement of handshapes across a keyboard instrument, where the geometry of the hand replaces the logic of tonality, is ultimately too hard a binary. Why cannot both ideas be thought to interact dialectically?

Furthermore, it is surely impossible to decide abstractly whether a chord is behaving in the manner of a 'voice-leading object' or an 'acoustic object'.[22] (This is the principal means through which Cohn distinguishes tonal from 'non-tonal' succession.) Smooth voice-leading might sometimes generate 'acoustic-style' progressions, and 'acoustic-style' progressions might be referenced (albeit in possibly distorted form) by parsimonious transformations. Philip Lambert's recent article on the behaviours of half-diminished-seventh chords helps to elucidate this point. He offers the four

Figure 4.3 Lambert (2021), Fig. 1, 'Four possible voice-leading models' (for the resolution of a ø⁷ chord). Reproduced by permission of Wiley.

following archetypes as a means of describing the resolution of a half-diminished seventh rooted on B; we focus on resolutions to V⁷s here, but Lambert's article deals with a number of other resolution chords too (see Figure 4.3):

> We associate the two wedging actions, W and X, with traditional harmonic resolutions, as in progressions from leading-note seventh or augmented sixth chords to their tonic- or dominant-functioning destinations.[23] In the fixed-tone models, Y and Z, however, the greater presence of common tones yields connections that are less dynamic and more metamorphic, as in progressions involving common-tone seventh chords or gradually unfolding harmonic mutations.[24]

Perhaps W and X motions might indicate (in addition to more standard V-I motions) moments in which [0258] chords 'hearken to their appellative properties after ignoring them for some measures'[25] (their having been engaged in Y and Z motions previously?). But consider the Hagen Chords, f♯ø⁷ to E♭⁷, discussed at the beginning of this chapter, which manifest a wedging motion, but which are also enharmonically paradoxical. Indeed, while W and X voice-leading types often imply kinship with tonal progressions, this is not always the case; many such progressions exhibit the kinds of ambiguities that might be seen to characterise Y and Z motions. (We will return to these chords, albeit as they appear in Waltraute's Plaint, later in the chapter, putting a Riemannian account of seventh chords into dialogue with an adapted depiction of Cohnian voice-leading space.)

What about Y and Z motions? Can their (non-)tonal behaviours be more easily generalised? We would argue 'no'. The tonal inferences of a move from bø⁷ either to C♯⁴₃ (Z) or to B⁷₄₃ (Y), for example, are still relatively clear (a modally mixed V⁴⁷⁶₅₃ dominant decoration in F♯⁺ or a chromaticised secondary dominant in °A), despite their parsimonious voice leading. The former and latter qualities are not mutually exclusive. Of course, Cohn invokes 4-Cube-Trio readings only when these parsimonious transformations are *chained*; but the point is that Z and Y motions do not defy tonal interpretation intrinsically – and we can only recognise that something has been chained retrospectively.

Cohn is aware of this point, of course, and demonstrates it admirably in his analysis of Chopin's Op. 28, No. 4. Considering a number of tonal readings of the prelude, by Schachter, Lehrdahl, and Gauldin, he discusses how they might interact productively with his 4-Cube Trio model. In particular, he focusses on how sevenths frequently do not resolve as one might expect them to, often for bars at a time. 'Each leading tone defies the summons and continues downward in a triumph of gravity and inertia over magnetism'.[26] But to interpret the chord progression in this way, he implies, is to define its logic negatively, in terms of tonal behaviours to which it does not ultimately conform. If one were to bundle all of these chained transformations together, then tonality defying enharmonic paradoxes would occur. But most undergraduates do not hear this music as being shot through with paradox – they hear it as tonal.

To refer back to a claim made earlier in this book (see p. 12):

> For there to be tonality on Riemann's understanding, very little is required .... If a piece of music contains triads, or chords that can be heard as combinations of triads, then there is tonality (one can almost hear Tonality saying: 'For where two or three triads are gathered together in my name, there I am in the midst of them').

One might say that Riemann is being ideological here. All the same, Riemann's approach seems closer to the impressions of twenty-first-century undergraduates than is Cohn here, if our own teaching experiences are anything to go by. No matter how hard we try to argue the case, students cannot accept that tonality has been abandoned in this prelude, at any point. If tonality lives in us, rather than residing abstractly in a Platonic world of forms, then it is at least worth trying to show how some of us might perceive music such as this to be tonal.

Simply to return to the traditional-style readings Cohn surveys, however, would clearly be inadequate: they do not come close to revealing the nuances that Cohn's approach models so brilliantly (e.g. counterpoint can be a useful means of explanation, but it generally explains only two of the four pitches in every chord). In what follows, we adapt the 4-Cube Trio in such a way that the smooth, chromatic universe it reveals is preserved, but that the chords contained therein are tonally *re*-oriented. Rather than seventh chords having an arbitrary position on the page, they are now explicitly oriented towards a T-S-D triangle (see Figure 4.4).

In this *Tristan*-esque environment, triads are understood to be relatively stable. When they acquire a seventh, however, they point beyond themselves to the next function, hence the colour-coding: $°T=°E$ and E7 (a tonic dissonance, henceforth T^{diss}, which points towards a triadic $°S$) both have white backgrounds; triadic $°S$ and S^{diss} have light grey backgrounds; and D and D^{diss} have dark grey backgrounds. (NB: Triads can be modified by Riemannian transformations, but these possibilities are not listed at the outset in order to

The Multiple Lives of Seventh Chords   65

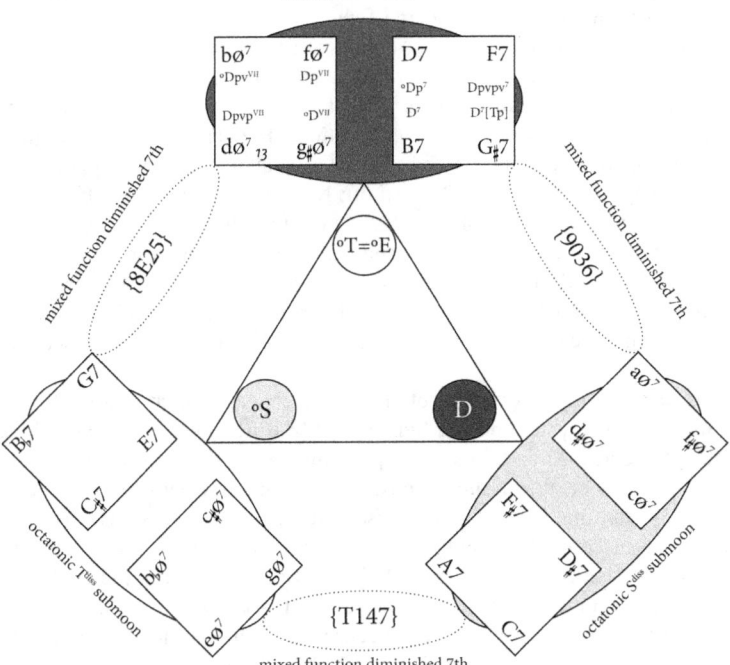

Figure 4.4 Octatonic submoon function graph, based on Cohn's 4-Cube Trio (refer back to Figure 4.2).

avoid clutter.) The ovals in which T^{diss}, S^{diss}, and D^{diss} chords are housed are conceptualised as 'submoons', which themselves orbit the moons of T, S, and D.

In Cohn's original 4-Cube Trio graph (refer back to Figure 4.2), the diminished sevenths form the principal nodes: they are generators of all the other V^7 and $Ø^7$ chords. In our graph, by contrast, [0369] chords – indicated by smaller ovals with dotted edges – serve as bridges between T^{diss}, S^{diss}, and D^{diss} functions. As Daniel Harrison has noted, diminished sevenths contain an equal number of dominant and subdominant scale degrees: i.e. two of each.[27] If the oval seventh-chord submoons that orbit the functional triangle are understood each to manifest a *single* function, albeit with varying degrees of strength, then the diminished sevenths can be understood to be split between *different* functions.

In consequence of this change, the four V^7 and $Ø^7$ chords in any one submoon are no longer equivocally related: i.e. they cannot be characterised as equally probable perturbations of the same fully diminished-seventh. Instead, the diatonic dominant is considered functionally prime (e.g. B7 in °E); the upper and lower mediants of that dominant are secondary functions (being brighter or darker, respectively, depending on their sharp- or flat-side status); and the primary D's tritonal counterpart manifests the most attenuated form of major-dominant function. A more conventional Riemannian account of these chords' triadic basis helps to clarify this interpretation: G♯⁺ = (D)[Tp] (2 semitones offset from the purest D function); D⁺ = °Dp (3 semitones offset from D); and F⁺ = Dp$_V$p$_V$ (6 semitones offset from D). The latter label, of course, is particularly strained, and only applies if F⁺ were to be heard as part of a movement *away* from a clearly articulated, normative D function. (Triadically speaking, F⁺ is much closer to °𝕊.) But the tritone-substitutional relationship between dominant-*sevenths* built on {B} and {F} guarantees their functional kinship.

Half-diminished versions of the same chords, which belong to the same octatonic scale and are thus arguably functionally equivalent, are interpreted according to a similar principle, except that they are notably weaker in affect. While they can be represented as voice-leading adjustments of dominant-functioning dissonances, as we shall shortly see, all Ø⁷ chords are potentially plagal in sound (i.e. they contain ♭6̂ of the next, anti-clockwise function), hence their positioning towards the S-side of whichever functional region they occupy. In °E, Ø⁷ chords in the D^{diss} submoon are ordered as follows, according to their functional potency: g♯ø⁷, °D^{VII} (1 semitone offset D); fø⁷, Dp^{VII} (2 semitones offset from D); bø⁷, °Dp$_V^{VII}$ (4 semitones offset from D); dø⁷, Dp$_V$p^{VII} (5 semitones offset from D). While all Ø⁷ chords within the same octatonic submoon are only two semitones removed from *one another*, we rank them instead in terms of their proximity to the *triadic dominant*, whose function they (potentially) extend. Indeed, while the functional 'meanings' of any of these chords are necessarily plural, *these chords are not likely to discharge in the usual, disjunct way, if a smooth voice-leading aesthetic is in force.* Rather, the listener may hear such progressions in terms of a slow movement away from the light-side of a particular functional submoon towards its dark-side, the music's becoming steadily enriched (or corrupted) as we begin to feel the tug of the gravitational field of another function. (NB: Dark-side is basically a synonym for functional extravagance.)

A concrete example will help to make these ideas clearer. In Chopin's Op. 28, No. 4, for example, the dominant seventh in b. 2, rather than discharging, is incrementally darkened: its 5̂ is flattened <F♯,F♮> (resulting in a French 6th), followed by 3̂, <D♯,D♮> (bØ⁷); 7̂ then moves to ♯6̂ (dØ⁷): see Figure 4.5 and Example 4.3.[28] This move towards the subdominant-side edge of D^{diss} is consolidated by a downshift to a new functional submoon;

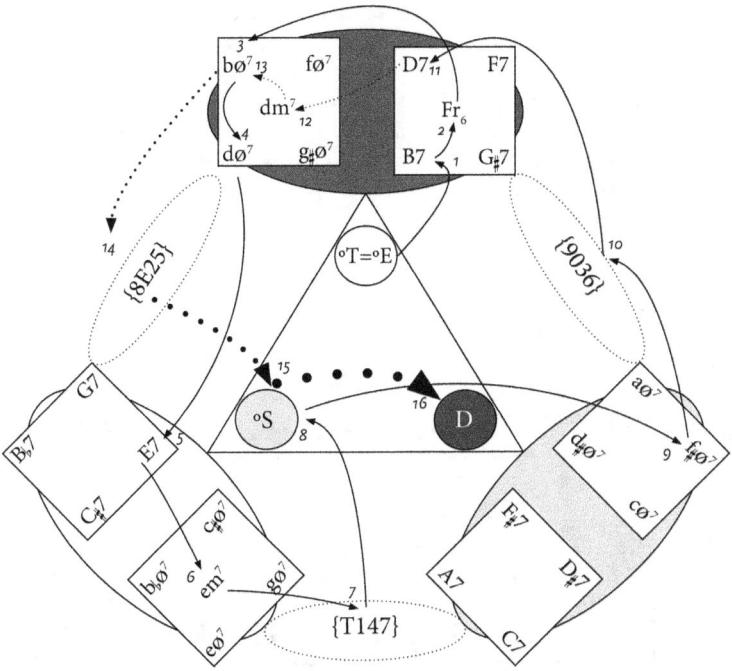

Figure 4.5 Chopin, Op. 28, No. 4, bb. 1–13 (octatonic submoon function graph). Step 16 marks a half-cadence.

the diatonic dominant of S, E7, is engaged. In the same way as the earlier B7, however, the scale degrees of this 'pure' dominant are depressed: first $\hat{3}$ <G♯,G> (eø⁷) and then $\hat{7}$ <D,C♯> (e°⁷). The latter chord is functionally ambiguous. In true Riemannian fashion, we might think of it either as Đ7⁹⁾ of F⁺ (°𝕊) or of B⁺ (D). °A, the subdominant, proves to be the temporary goal, but no sooner have we alighted on it than an under third is added: a characteristic dissonance that immediately points this chord towards the next function. Another polyvalent diminished-seventh is then articulated, before a further anti-clockwise move round the space to D⁺7. To us, this chord feels marked; special. It pulses for a whole bar, halving the previously established rate of harmonic change. Having passed round to the back of the dominant moon, the tonic has come back into view; we have returned to the D^diss submoon that contained the phrase's originating B7. Cohn's 4-Cube Trio representation of the prelude also highlights this moment. But the return is marked as a return to a neutral node in

68 *The Multiple Lives of Seventh Chords*

a decentred space; there is no sense that a weaker but related dominant function has been reasserted.[29] A further rotation then takes place (see the dotted arrows in Figure 4.5). This is much more direct; its functional journey is more focussed. It is as if Chopin has *just* missed the dominant he was aiming for; the next journey round functional space is thus more impatient, more resolute (NB: the dotted arrows become larger as a clear functional resolution comes into view).

Example 4.2 The antecedent phrase of Chopin's Op. 28, No. 4, bb. 1–12, with Riemannian overlay.

Non-Parsimonious, Non-Conventional Seventh-Chord Relations

There are some forms of tetrachordal relationship that are neither parsimonious nor diatonic: they are thus unconducive to a neo- or an original-Riemannian worldview. In particular, conventional Riemannian analysis, which reduces sevenths to triads, might seem to produce too many functional options for a particular chromatic chord for it to be of clear use. Our octatonic submoon system provides a means of clarifying and disciplining these functions.

The Multiple Lives of Seventh Chords 69

To demonstrate, let us return to the Hagen chords with which this chapter began, albeit considering now how they are redeployed in a later section of Waltraute's Plaint (see Example 4.3).

Example 4.3 The 'Hagen chords' as part of Waltraute's Plaint, *Götterdämmerung*, Act 1, Scene 3, bb. 1296–310.

What is the relationship between aø⁷ and F♯⁷, if we take the latter as a tonic with an added seventh (NB: much of the Plaint is grounded in F♯)? To answer this question, we must first consider what species of extension {A,C,E♭,G} is: that is, either a dominant ninth with an omitted root (F⁹) or a minor triad with an underthird (°C^VII). Each of these possibilities would itself have multiple possible functional designations. F⁹, reduced to a simpler, triadic form, could be either 𝔻p_v or 𝔅_v; °C^VII, again, reduced to a simpler triadic form, could be

70 The Multiple Lives of Seventh Chords

either °T$_{p^v p^v}$ or ⌀. One might throw one's hands up in despair at this point: orthodoxly Riemannian interpretation seems to result in hopelessly prolix labels that bear little relation to the objects that they describe. Let us modulate into a different, *neo*-Riemannian world, and examine these chords as they appear on a 4-Cube Trio (refer back to Figure 4.2). While aø^7 and F♯^{7} form part of the same octatonic pool (indeed, they exhaust the octatonic aggregate), the voice leading between them is not exactly smooth (four semitones cumulatively), even if each voice moves smoothly in isolation. It would appear that neither method, new nor old, can account for Wagner's 'farfetched Effect'.

The octatonic-submoon diagram below (Figure 4.6), however, facilitates greater specificity, and a dialectical mediation between the two methods. Lying towards the edge of the T^{diss} region, aø^7 is precarious, its being incestuously close to the S/𝔻^{diss} domain. Two of Riemann's hypothetical labels, °T$_{p^v p^v}^{VII}$ and ⌀^{VII}, which might previously have seemed untenable, are seemingly vindicated[30];

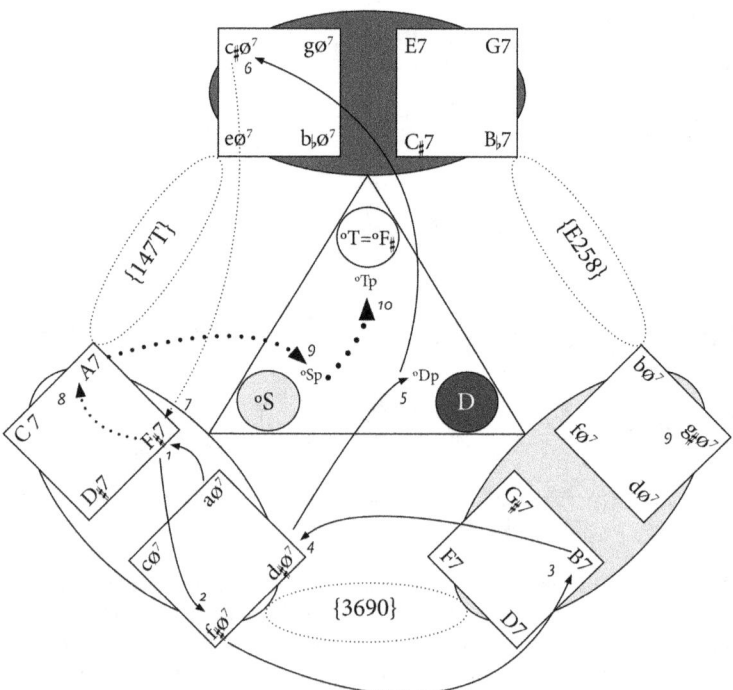

Figure 4.6 Waltraute's Plaint, *Götterdämmerung*, Act 1, Scene 3, bb. 1296–310, octatonic submoon function graph.

but we now have a spatial, graphic means of deciding which of these functions is the stronger: i.e. we can determine which 'region' a chord is in, but see also how proximate it is to others, thus accounting for its relatively pure or mixed function. What is perhaps most illuminating about this is that °Tp,p̌^{VII} has more modifiers than ⓇⅤ^{II}, which would ordinarily lead us to think of the latter label as being more plausible. Our octatonic-submoon diagram makes it possible to argue precisely the opposite: the chord's overall function is definitively tonic, while being considerably influenced by the gravity of 𝔻^{dim}.

In short, Riemann's method of dealing with sevenths has huge advantages, but it sometimes lacks the clarity of an NRT representation of tetrachords (particularly the ways in which the latter accounts for smooth voice leading). By making a return to Riemann from the music-theoretical present, we argue that one can have one's analytical cake and eat it: we can capture the voice-leading and functional characteristics of these chords and their relations in an eye-catching and efficient way, staying true to Riemann's principles, while taking account of Cohn's well-made criticisms.

Notes

1 Richard Wagner, *Richard Wagner's Prose Works, Vol. VI: Religion and Art*, trans. William Ashton Ellis (London: Kegan Paul, Trench, Trübner & Co, Ltd., 1897), 188.
2 One could interpret this either as Ð^9-T or as Sp^{VII}-T, depending on whether an over- or undertonal perspective was adopted. Given the gold's belonging to the family of Nature motifs, based on *ascending* arpeggiation, we suggest that the former label is more appropriate.
3 Philip Lambert, 'Half-Diminished Seventh Chords and Their Contexts', *Music Analysis* 39, no. 3 (2021): 277–313, 280.
4 Rings uses this diagram to capture the ways in which scale degrees (the x axis) and pitch classes (the y axis) relate to one another, and to point up moments where they converge and/or diverge. See Steven Rings, *Tonality and Transformation* (Oxford: Oxford University Press, 2011), 83–8.
5 It is the possibility of multiple scale-degree designations that makes this leitmotif enharmonically paradoxical. As William Benjamin has pointed out, '[in the] theoretical universe [of NRT] a key cannot include two spellings of the same pitch class as elements of triads [or sevenths]': William Benjamin, 'Review: *The Oxford Handbook of Neo-Riemannian Music Theories* by Edward Gollin, Alexander Rehding', *Journal of Music Theory* 58, no. 2 (2014): 235–56, 253.
6 Hugo Riemann, *Harmony Simplified; Or, The Theory of the Tonal Functions of Chords*, trans. unknown (London: Augner Ltd., 1896 [1893]), 55–61.
7 See Richard Cohn, *Audacious Euphony: Chromaticism and the Triad's Second Nature* (Oxford: Oxford University Press, 2012), 149.
8 Ibid., 150; our emphases.
9 Ibid., xiii.
10 Oliver Chandler, '"Octatonic" Voice Leading and Diatonic Function: the Finale of Elgar's String Quartet op. 83', *Music Theory Online* 26, no. 1 (2020). https://mtosmt.org/issues/mto.20.26.1/mto.20.26.1.chandler.html.
11 We use pitch-class set notation for these chords because of the redundancy of their possible enharmonic spellings for a diagram that obeys essentially post-tonal principles: see Figure 4.2.

12 Delimited because if you chain enough transformations together, they will eventually lead back to the same starting point: i.e. the space's extension is finite.
13 Daniel Harrison, 'Three Short Essays on Neo-Riemannian Theory', in *The Oxford Handbook to Neo-Riemannian Music Theories*, eds. Alexander Rehding and Steven Rings (Oxford: Oxford University Press, 2011), 548–78, 550, 551.
14 Ibid., 552.
15 *Audacious Euphony*, 186; our emphasis.
16 Cohn has stressed to us that this aspect of his work has often been overlooked, thus transforming the possibilities he envisages and reifying them into prescriptive 'oughts': personal communication, 1 April 2020.
17 Cohn, *Audacious Euphony*, 186.
18 Hyer, 'Reimag(in)ing Riemann', *Journal of Music Theory* 39, no. 1 (1995): 101–38, 128.
19 Cohn, *Audacious Euphony*, 165: e.g. If we call something F♯7, it implies only one possible key, namely B. If it resolved to F7, we would be dealing with a German 6th, not an F♯7 chord, etc.
20 Ibid., 186.
21 Ibid.
22 Ibid., 188.
23 Lambert notes that these W and X motions may no longer exemplify contrary motion to a resolution chord when a seventh is added to the latter: 'Half-Diminished Seventh Chords', 290.
24 Ibid., 280.
25 Cohn, *Audacious Euphony*, 157.
26 Ibid., 162.
27 Daniel Harrison, *Harmonic Function in Chromatic Music: A Renewed Dualist Theory and an Account of Its Precedents* (Chicago: University of Chicago Press, 1994), 64–9.
28 We follow the convention in pitch-class theory here of using <angle brackets> to show an ordered pitch succession.
29 Richard Cohn, animated analysis of Chopin's Op. 28, No. 4 using a 4-Cube Trio, Web Figure 7.25
 https://global.oup.com/us/companion.websites/9780199772698/resources/chapt7/7_25/.
30 Dp_v and D_v, by contrast, may be dismissed: the former replicates the same general function as D_v, and the latter seems disconnected from a^o7's positioning on the submoon graph.

Bibliography

Benjamin, William. 'Review: *The Oxford Handbook of Neo-Riemannian Music Theories* by Edward Gollin, Alexander Rehding', *Journal of Music Theory* 58, no. 2 (2014): 235–56.

Chandler, Oliver. '"Octatonic" Voice Leading and Diatonic Function: The finale of Elgar's String Quartet Op. 83', *Music Theory Online* 26, no. 1 (2020). https://mtosmt.org/issues/mto.20.26.1/mto.20.26.1.chandler.html

Cohn, Richard. *Audacious Euphony: Chromaticism and the Triad's Second Nature*. Oxford: Oxford University Press, 2012.

———. 'Animated Analysis of Chopin's Op. 28, No. 4 using a 4-Cube Trio', Web Figure 7.25. *Audacious Euphony: Chromaticism and the Triad's Second Nature*.

Oxford: Oxford University Press, 2012. https://global.oup.com/us/companion.websites/9780199772698/resources/chapt7/7_25/.

Harrison, Daniel. *Harmonic Function in Chromatic Music: A Renewed Dualist Theory and an Account of Its Precedents.* Chicago: Chicago University Press, 1994.

———. 'Three Short Essays on Neo-Riemannian Theory', in *The Oxford Handbook to Neo-Riemannian Music Theories,* edited by Alexander Rehding, and Steven Rings, 548–78. Oxford: Oxford University Press, 2011.

Hyer, Bryan. 'Reimag(in)ing Riemann', *Journal of Music Theory* 39, no. 1 (1995): 101–38.

Lambert, Philip. 'Half-Diminished Seventh Chords and Their Contexts', *Music Analysis* 39, no. 3 (2021): 277–313.

Riemann, Hugo. *Harmony Simplified; Or, The Theory of the Tonal Functions of Chords*, translated unknown London: Augner Ltd., 1893 [1896].

Rings, Steven. *Tonality and Transformation.* Oxford: Oxford University Press, 2011.

Wagner, Richard. *Richard Wagner's Prose Works, Vol. VI: Religion and Art*, translated by William Ashton Ellis. London: Kegan Paul, Trench, Trübner & Co, Ltd, 1897.

5 'Here Time Becomes Space'
Schenkerising Riemann/Riemannising Schenker

In his analysis of the Prologue to *Götterdämmerung*, Patrick McCreless argues that the music of the first and second Norns – characters who reflect on the past and the present of the tetralogy – can be understood to compose-out normative diatonic contrapuntal structures in a way amenable to Schenkerian representation. The third Norn's music, however, which looks towards the future, 'loses its tonal-prolongational character while maintaining its linear character'.[1] This difference in pitch-organisation is prophetic: the collapse of the world of Wotan and the Gods is mirrored by the breakdown of the language of Austro-German classicism.

Figure 5.1 reproduces a section of McCreless's reading of the third Norn's music. The middle ground analysis, shown in the reproduction's first and second systems, reveals an overarching functional bass movement from <B-E>. On the surface, however, linear motions abound that do not compose-out a single vertical entity: e.g. the fifth progressions from <B-F> in soprano and bass connect B^+ to $D\flat^{+}_{3}$ (see the bottom two systems). While the root of the former chord can be understood, at a stretch, as the seventh of the latter, it is not literally present as an extension on the surface. Furthermore, it does not resolve in the way one might expect an unfolded seventh to resolve: $D\flat$ ultimately progresses to $f^{\varnothing 7}$; the prolonged F in the bass is decorated by a neighbour-note G (i.e. the root of a G7 chord). No diatonic harmony is being unfolded here; the horizontal dimension appears to have emancipated itself from the vertical. McCreless concludes that this kind of freely chromatic music is best regarded as 'an assemblage of tonalities that are symbols for dramatic elements, tonalities either briefly stated or convincingly tonicised, lined up into patterns of rising half-steps or falling third steps'.[2] We are on the cusp of a new world.

While this hermeneutic angle is attractive, we argue that it overestimates the music's resistance to quasi-Schenkerian enquiry. Wagner's melodic lines still reference vertical harmonies lying beneath the music's surface, even if some of these harmonies require interpretation in Riemannian (as opposed to Schenkerian) terms if their prolongational potential is to be understood.

DOI: 10.4324/9781003183655-6

'Here Time Becomes Space' 75

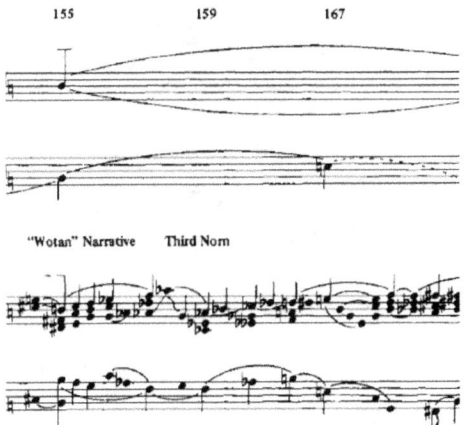

Figure 5.1 A section of McCreless's Schenkerian reading of the Prologue from *Götterdämmerung* (Example 11.3 in the original, p. 293); systems 1 & 3 are written in treble clef; systems 2 & 4 in bass clef. Reproduced by permission of University of California Press.

Our basic claim asserted, we shall now navigate a three-stage course. First, we offer a fairly orthodox reinterpretation of the passage McCreless analyses, freely supplementing his Schenkerian notations with Riemannian functions wherever necessary. Second, we consider a major methodological tension between Riemannian and Schenkerian systems – namely, the difference between *Stufen* and *Funktion* – and adapt Schenkerian notation to prioritise the latter aspect. And finally, we analyse a near-one-hundred-bar excerpt from *Götterdämmerung*, Act 1, Scene 3, in order to give an expanded context for the analyses of the same operatic act in previous chapters.

Schenkerian Notation with Supplementary Riemannian Labels

Consider McCreless' <B-F> fourth progression in bb. 155–8 once more, the terminal note of which is prolonged by an <F,G,F> neighbour note. To us, bb. 159–60 – the moment in which the third Norn sings 'Wotan im Saal' – feels like a ♭$\hat{2}$-$\hat{1}$ resolution onto G (see Example 5.1); it is {G} that is consonant, not {F}. One might wonder whether D♭⁺-G⁺ can function as meaningful harmonic support for said resolution; but one can understand the {F} in the bass as a neighbour to the bass {Gs} in bb. 157 and 160, respectively. This kind

76   'Here Time Becomes Space'

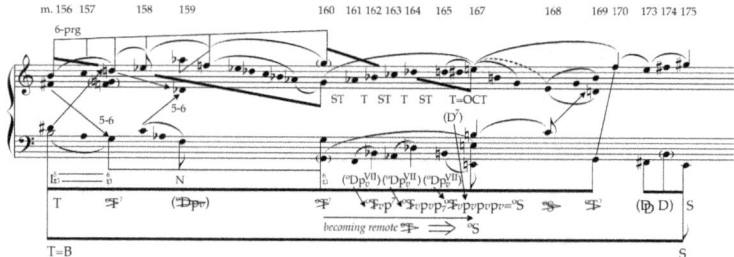

Figure 5.2 A Schenkerian *cum* Riemannian interpretation of *Götterdämmerung*, Prologue, bb. 156–75.

of lower-neighbour prolongation is usually dominant-functioning, at least in common-practice harmony; we can thus understand $D\flat^+$ – on the basis of its contrapuntal behaviour – as ($^*\text{Dp}_v$)G^+: see Figure 5.2.

Example 5.1 $\flat\hat{2}$-$\hat{1}$ vocal resolution, *Götterdämmerung*, Prologue, bb. 156–60.

But how should we understand G major? Abstractly, the label °Sp might be thought to make the most sense; but again, we must concern ourselves with the chord's contrapuntal context. In bb. 156–7, for example, B major

'Here Time Becomes Space' 77

is expanded by means of a 5-6 shift (with G major representing the tonic's chromatically modified '6-phase').[3] It thus makes sense to think of G as an extension of the tonic, which is then prolonged by a neighbouring bass motion.

We are now in a position to reconsider the upper line, too. Whereas McCreless draws his slur from <B-F>, we suggest that it continues implicitly to {G} – this note being displaced down an octave in the sounding music – as part of the broader composing-out of G⁺, a tonic substitute. Given the focus on G⁺ in our reading, the <F,A♭,B♮> bass arpeggiation highlighted by McCreless is no longer given the same importance, either. The Ø⁷'s that form it are interpreted instead as applied °Dp$_v^{vii}$s in relation to the nodes that they 'tonicise': namely, <B♭+,D♭+,°E>. Our 'tonic-substitutional' G⁺ can be grouped with this minor-third cycle to reveal the unfolding of a fully diminished-seventh. Note that the melody which this bassline supports is fundamentally octatonic, alternating semitones and tones. As argued in previous chapters, chords that belong to one octatonic scale generally have the same function. But there seems to be a tension here: Can the final °E really be understood as a T substitute when it has exactly the same note content as °S? Unlikely: °E is °S. On this logic, though, would not G⁺ be °Sp? Abstractly, this is indeed a possibility. As already discussed, however, because G⁺ was first introduced by means of a chromaticised 5-6 motion, it was heard originally as °𝐓. But a chord's meaning might change depending on one's temporal vantage point. We use Thomas Kul Kirkegaard-Larsen's typology here (⟹), adapted from Janet Schmalfeldt, to indicate that a chord's function changes over time. When G⁺ is arpeggiated as part of the diminished-seventh unfolding, for example, the initial hexatonic °𝐓 function is incrementally corrupted: i.e. °𝐓$_v$p, °𝐓$_v$p$_v$p, °𝐓$_v$p$_v$p$_v$. This 'becoming remote' allows the initial function of the chord to melt away, changing seamlessly from °T to °S: i.e. °𝐓$_v$p$_v$p$_v$ ⟹ °S. After °E is expanded by a 5-6 shift (°$), we resolve plagally back to yet another G7 chord, itself pressing on once more to the subdominant: i.e. °𝐓⁷ (𝐃-D)S. (Note how different our slurring is from that of McCreless: e.g. while he shows the upper-voice E at b. 167 as a mere passing note, we render it as the goal of the progression.) Crucially, though, this subdominant is more stable, and the Schenkerian notation allows us to distinguish between a surface °S event – attached to the shallowest beam, in b. 167 – and one that manifests at a deeper structural level – attached to the deepest beam, in b. 175.

An Adapted Schenkerian Notation

We hope that the preceding analysis, which combined Schenkerian and Riemannian insights in a pragmatic, non-systematic way, was reasonably successful; but, it ultimately disguises a major point of tension between the two

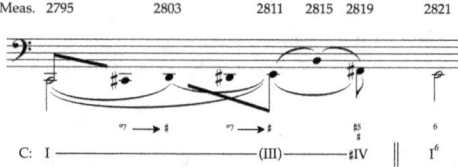

Figure 5.3 Darcy's bass-voice reading of Wagner's *Das Rheingold*, Scene 3, bb. 2795–821 (1996: 182, Ex. 10.1). Reproduced by permission of Oxford University Press.

theoretical approaches: namely, the difference between '*Stufe*' [scale-step] and 'function'. In the case of a 5-6 shift, for example, the '6-phase' harmony might have a different *sounding* root to the chord that it elaborates, but it belongs, conceptually, to one and the same fundamental bass tone: i.e. the root of the '5-phase' chord. *Stufe* and 'function' do not interfere with one another in circumstances such as this: they both refer to chords of 'tonic' quality, rooted conceptually on the same pitch. But in some circumstances, they *do* interfere with one another. Take the following bassline reduction from Warren Darcy's book, *Wagner's Das Rheingold* (Figure 5.3).

Darcy writes that this graph 'displays a rather unorthodox interruption structure: the interruption occurs after the pre-dominant harmony (♯IV) rather than the usual dominant'.[4] Scale-step theory – the idea that every chord is necessarily built on one of the degrees, natural or chromatically altered, of a major or minor scale – means that we are left with little choice but to interpret this chord as ♯IV. (If we were to call it ♭$\hat{5}$, then we would condemn the leading-tone of the dominant to be synonymous with the dominant it aims to tonicise.) ♯$\hat{4}$ is implicitly associated with pre-dominant function: e.g. in C major, {F♯} often rises to {G}, $\hat{5}$, as the root of a dominant chord. But that does not happen here: {F♯} 'falls' to {E} (the latter pitch being transposed up the octave in the actual music). Interpreting this moment as a 'deformed' interruption does little to clarify its effect: $\hat{2}$ appears to be part of an upwards passing motion; it does not figure as the penultimate station of a teleological descent. Let us temporarily jettison the idea that this chord is ♯IV, and focus instead on how it *functions*.

Darcy's bass reduction picks out four central nodes <C,E,F♯,C> in bb. 2795–821, which are connected either by passing motions, i.e. <C,[C♯,D,D♯],E>, or an interpolated dominant, i.e. <E,[B],F♯>. In functional terms, we can conceptualise these nodes as T, $\mathfrak{T}_v$, Tp$_v$p$_v$, and T. In other words, there is a sense of moving away from a 'pure' tonic function towards one that is maximally enriched, before returning once again to that function's purest (albeit now inverted) form. For us, the progression is not characterised by a feeling of external interruption, but of continuous movement away from, and then back towards, a central point: almost like the stretching and springing

Figure 5.4 A Schenkerian *cum* Riemannian interpretation of *Das Rheingold*, Scene 3, bb. 2795–821.

back of an elastic cord. We attempt to capture this graphically through a modified Schenkerian notation (Figure 5.4).

C⁺ is represented by a breve: it is the 'purest' (or 'lightest') form of Tonic function. E⁺, by contrast, is shown as a minim with a cross through it: it is *two* transformations away from T. (An ordinary minim head would have been used had the chord in question been only *one* transformation away from T: e.g. °E.) F♯⁺ is represented only by a cross: this captures its distance from, but ultimate functional similarity to, the originating tonic: it is a dark-side function. All notes that serve to prolong these middle ground notes – i.e. the <C,[C♯,D,D♯],E> linear progression or the <E,[B],F♯> interpolated dominant – are shown using conventional stemless crotchets, in the standard Schenkerian manner.

By trading in *Stufen* for functions, we can understand the way in which Wagner prolongs a single function over time – namely, Tonic – but in such a way that we can also track its changing affective qualities (i.e. light- or dark-side). We are still able to understand the music's contrapuntal dimension, however, through the retention (albeit in adapted, Riemannian form) of Darcy's Schenkerian notation: we do not limit ourselves to mapping moment-to-moment changes of chord. This represents one of the most fundamental of Darcy's insights: namely, that Wagner's music *does* build recursively. It is not the case here, as Dahlhaus argued more generally, that 'keys, or fragmentary allusions to keys, do not always relate to a constant centre [in Wagner's music] ... but should rather be seen as joined together like the links in a chain, without there necessarily being any other connection between the first and third links than the second'.⁵ It is not our intention to argue with Dahlhaus *in toto*; his approach remains an invaluable way of conceiving of Wagnerian tonality. But we think that it is also useful to consider how the tonal/harmonic relations in a Wagner scene might compose-out a broader functional *whole*. If tonality is a totalising ideology – as we have argued it is – then we need a means of *representing* that whole.

A Middle-Ground Analysis of Waltraute's Plaint

We will now test our novel notation on Waltraute's plaint. In the process, we give a broader middle-ground context for those excerpts we have already analysed in the book. To recap briefly: we use normal Schenkerian notation to represent local events (i.e. prolongational spans; small-scale cadences),

80 'Here Time Becomes Space'

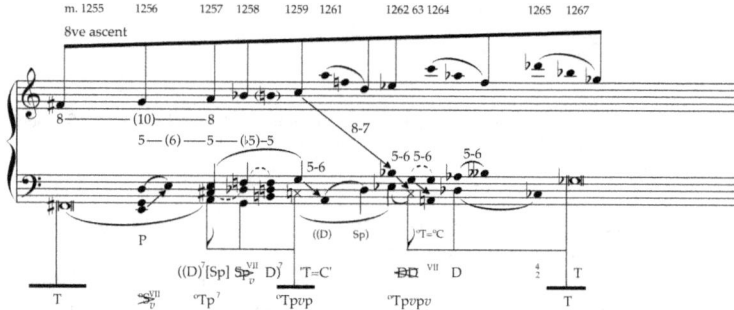

Figure 5.5 A Schenkerian *cum* Riemannian interpretation of *Götterdämmerung*, Act 1, Scene 3, bb. 1255–67.

but we interpret middle-ground tonicisations using our adapted Riemannian apparatus, in order to show functional continuity or change. Different kinds of notehead are used to represent tonicised middle-ground harmonies: breves symbolise 'pure', diatonic functions; open note heads signify a minimally altered diatonic function (i.e. one semitone or tone of remove); open note heads with a cross indicate a chromatic function with two alterations; and crosses on their own indicate a 'dark-side' function (i.e. more than two alterations).

We will now demonstrate these principles in action: first, at a surface level and, then, a middle-ground level. Looking at Figure 5.5 (bb. 1255–67), for example, it can be seen that F♯⁺ is initially prolonged by means of a mode-changing third progression. (The underthird, {E}, which decorates the passing °G, prevents parallel octaves.) The resultant A⁺, however, has a double function. Not only does it prolong F♯⁺; its root also functions as a neighbour note to a dominant in C⁺ (°Tᵥp).

We believe that this approach to bb. 1255–9 has three principal benefits:

1. *An excessively local harmonic perspective is traded in for something more melodically sensitive. This, in turn, reveals a broader harmonic process: a movement from light- to dark-side tonal function.* For example, a more conventional Riemannian account of this progression – °F♯ °G^VII A7 °B♭^VII G7 C – might be °T °S̸ᵥ^VII °T_P^7 = ((D⁷) [Sp] S̸P_ᵥ^VII D⁷) °Tᵥp. Arguably, this captures better the 'in the moment' feeling of tension and release immanent in the progression's sequential aspect, while still remaining monotonal. But it does not account for the progression's specific counterpoint. For example, the °S̸ᵥ^VII is a contrapuntal chord that prolongs a move from °T to °T_P^7; it does not suggest a strong function, in and of itself. While the move from A7 to °B♭^VII can be interpreted locally as a deceptive cadence, the broader context, we argue, suggests

that this progression serves instead as an unusual means of breaking parallel fifths: A/E-G/D becomes A/E-(G/D♭)-G/D. (The more conventional fifth-breaking formula, 5-(6)-5, is sublated by this Wagnerian variant.) When graphed in this way, a general enrichment (or corruption) of the opening tonic – °T→°Tp̃→°Tp_vp – becomes more readily apparent.

2. *The manner in which each T-representative is tonicised is represented alongside, and is shown to interact with, the broader melodic lines that the music traces.* The soprano ascent, from $\hat{1}$-♭$\hat{5}$, and from ♭$\hat{5}$-$\hat{8}$, for example, would not be considered prolongational from a traditionally Schenkerian perspective: the first and last notes of these motions do not belong harmonically to their goal harmonies: C and G♭, respectively. Daniel Harrison calls lines like this, which are linear but not prolongational, Hindemith lines.[6] But we believe that the Riemannian functional kinship these chords can be argued to exhibit gives these ascending tritones a genuinely functional force. It is worth noting, though, that these melodic lines do not carry the structural weight of an *Urlinie*. We are attempting to demonstrate that this music can function melodically and prolongationally, not that it adheres to all parameters outlined in Schenker's *Free Composition*.

3. *The errant need not be rationalised by the presence of imaginary pitches;* {C} *does not have to be interpreted as a neighbour note to an absent dominant,* {C♯} *(as it would be on the basis of a* Stufe *perspective).* While its qualitative difference from the pure, diatonic version of the function is clearly foregrounded – it is recognised as a dark-side function, as indicated by the cross-notehead – it can still be shown to belong to the same functional category. From the perspective of Wagnerian rhetorical dialectics, this innovation is vital. The leitmotifs encountered during this passage – chromatically modified iterations of the Valhalla motif – convey the bewilderment of the heroes in their heavenly home, as Wotan commands them to heap the severed limbs of the World Ash Tree around the foundations of the fortress, in preparation for its immolation. The motive's glory is still in evidence, but it is placed at various degrees of ironic remove by and through chromatic manipulation.

Between bb. 1259–61, C⁺ is elaborated by a chromatically modified 5-6 shift, which tonicises D minor; the root of the latter chord is a passing note connecting {C} to {E♭}. E♭⁺, in turn, represents an $\hat{8}$-$\hat{7}$ elaboration of °C. A strained cadential formula is then sounded: °Tp_vp$_v$-Ð^{VII}-D-T. Overall, we can understand bb. 1255–67 to manifest a strange form of tonic prolongation: a cumulative process of tonic darkening and brightening.

Figure 5.6 presents the music already examined in Figure 5.5 as part of a broader middleground argument, running from bb. 1255–341. Here is the libretto for the music that this graph summarises:

82 'Here Time Becomes Space'

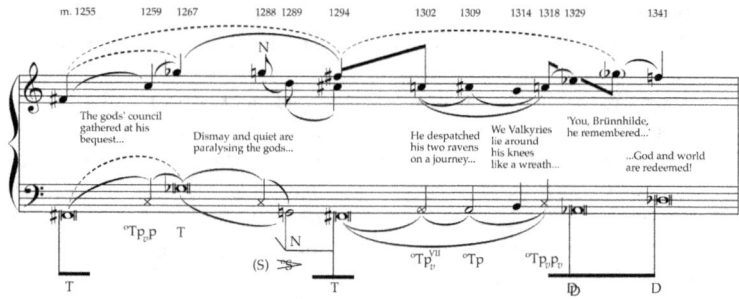

Figure 5.6 A Schenkerian *cum* Riemannian interpretation of *Götterdämmerung*, Act 1, Scene 3, bb. 1255–341.

The logs of the trunk / he ordered to be piled / in soaring stacks / around the sacred hall. The god's council / gathered at his behest; / solemnly he took his place on the throne: / he asked the troubled gods / to sit on either side of him, / as the heroes filled the hall / in circles and in rows. / There he sits / on his august seat, / voiceless and unsmiling, / no word from his lips; / the spear's broken pieces / tightly in his hand; / no longer touching / Holda's apples. / Dismay and disquiet / are paralysing the gods. He despatched his two ravens on a journey; / if they should ever come back with good news; - then just once more – for the last time! – the god would smile for ever. We Valkyries lie around / his knees like a wreath, - / he stays blind / to our beseeching gaze: / consuming us all / are our faint hearts and endless fear. - / Crying, I pressed myself close to his breast; - / his expression softened a little; - / you, Brünnhilde, he remembered! / He let out a deep sigh, / closed his eye, / and murmured these words / as if in a dream: / 'if she returns the ring to the Rhine / and the daughters in its depths, - / god and world are redeemed from the burden of the curse!'[7]

As can be seen from the graph, bb. 1255–67, defined by an <F♯-G♭> octave ascent in upper voice and bass, contrasts the affirmative power of Valhalla (associated with F♯/G♭⁺, the purest form of tonic function) and the fear of its agents (C⁺, a distant tonic function). Bars 1267–94 are similarly static, because of the <F♯,G,F♯> neighbour-note progression in the upper voice and in the bass: 'Dismay and disquiet / are paralysing the gods'. But tonic function soon becomes more protean. In bb. 1294–309, T becomes °Tp$_V^{VII}$ becomes °Tp: Wotan's ravens leave Valhalla, searching for good news (the end of the curse); a sense of renewed hope is felt. The move to C⁺, though – bright but at a maximal functional distance from the original F♯⁺ – further accentuates Waltraute's desperation at the situation. When Waltraute relays Wotan's remembering of Brünnhilde, however – the agent of resolution for the whole tetralogy – we see the first *genuinely functional change*: i.e. to 𝔻, and then to D. This represents a fundamental development in the drama: agency passes from Wotan to Brünnhilde. Rather than being incidental to the action on stage, tonality's functioning across this 86-bar span is vital. It registers an initially static but tortured state of affairs – the anxious suspense of Valhalla's heroes – and the conflicted substance of Valhalla itself, both ideal and sordid. But it also mimes the changing relationship between the tetralogy's characters in a profound way. Middle-ground functional rotation augurs the emergence of Brünnhilde, heroine.

Provisional Conclusions

We believe that the hybrid Schenkerian/Riemannian apparatus modelled in the previous sections offers possible solutions to a number of problems in the analysis of late-tonal music. On a practical level, NRT-inspired graphic systems – Cohn's hexatonic cycles, our functional (sub)moon graphs, etc. – can be overlaid only with a certain number of annotations before one stops being able to see the wood for the trees. An adapted Schenkerian notation, by contrast, allows us to represent in detail far broader musical spans with relative ease. On a theoretical level, the prospective mode of musical engagement that Riemann implicitly advocates can carry us only so far; it is difficult to get beyond rich descriptions of atomistic moments. Schenker's emphasis on musical retrospection, by contrast, allows one to see how a series of seemingly radical events might ultimately compose-out a systematically explainable (and thus ideologically mediated) whole.[8] Combining these approaches allows us to understand better how a chromatic chord might function, both in the moment and in its broader context(s). Crucially, however, our Riemannian conception of tonality is far less prescriptive than is Schenker's, while still being delimited: any chord can be given a function, but there is a clear distinction between that which functions normatively, in a light-side fashion, and that which functions errantly, in a dark-side capacity. The spectrum between these extremes is subtle yet quantifiable.

In the preface to this book, we wrote that 'tonality is an ideology of such sophistication and resilience that it would take a stronger force than that exerted by the post-Wagnerians to tear it apart. [… It] is an ideology of *totality*, in which the central idea explains everything' (p. 2). Rather than defining tonality theoretically, in terms of necessary and sufficient conditions, we have sought to explain it culturally. Late tonal music did not emerge from the post-modern relativism of our own epoch, but rather during a time in which grand narratives became so overinflated that they began to break down. (Indeed, Wagner's *Ring*, on which much of the analysis of this book has been focussed, is arguably the *locus classicus* of this trend.) Tonality is thus metalogically akin to a societal belief system that is still in force yet under great strain. But while we might have defined the phenomenon of tonality culturally, we have sought to explain its operation technically. Constellations of functional (sub)moons and the broader fields of function that emerge in our hybrid Riemannian/Schenkerian system have enabled us to demonstrate how tonal functions operate in some of the most densely chromatic music of the late nineteenth century. We have attempted to remain true to how Wagnerian-style tonality *feels*, while also offering reasonably concrete limits for functional ascription. If Wagner located the human world somewhere between the celestial lightness of Valhalla and the oppressive darkness of Nibelheim, this book has sought to show how tonality – a societal model sedimented in musical materials – is caught in a state of constant dialectical tension between light-side-diatonic and dark-side-chromatic functions. The latter, crucially, do not represent a new, utopian order of chromatic democracy, but rather a determinate negation of tonal hierarchy. 'The dissonances have assumed the character of sovereign subjectivity vis-à-vis the resolutions: they protest against the right of a social authority to make the rules', while ultimately remaining subject to them.[9]

Notes

1 Patrick McCreless, 'Schenker and the Norns', in *Analyzing Opera: Verdi and Wagner*, eds. Carolyn Abbate and Roger Parker (Berkeley: University of California Press, 1989), 276–97, 291.
2 Ibid., 288.
3 David Damschroder, *Tonal Analysis: A Schenkerian Perspective* (New York: W. W. Norton, 2018), 259.
4 Warren Darcy, *Wagner's Das Rheingold* (Oxford: Oxford University Press, 1993), 183.
5 Carl Dahlhaus, 'Issues in Composition', in *Between Romanticism and Modernism: Four Studies in the Music of the Later Nineteenth Century*, trans. Mary Whittall (Berkeley: University of California Press, 1980), 65–75.
6 Daniel Harrison, *Pieces of Tradition: An Analysis of Contemporary Tonal Music* (Oxford: Oxford University Press, 2016), 83.
7 Richard Wagner, *The Ring of the Nibelung*, trans. and ed., John Deathridge (London: Penguin Books, 2018), 595, 597.
8 We have been much influenced on the subject of temporality in Schenker's and Riemann's theories by Thomas Jul Kirkegaard-Larsen's *Analytical Practices in Western Music Theory: A Comparison and Mediation of Schenkerian and Post-Riemannian Traditions* (Ph.D. diss.: Aarhus University, 2020), 288–96.
9 Theodor W. Adorno, *In Search of Wagner*, trans. Rodney Livingstone (London: Verso, 1981), 54–5.

Bibliography

Adorno, Theodor W. *In Search of Wagner*, translated by Rodney Livingstone. London: Verso, 1981.

Dahlhaus, Carl. *Between Romanticism and Modernism: Four Studies in the Music of the Later Nineteenth Century*, translated by Mary Whittall. Berkeley and Los Angeles, 1980.

Damschroder, David. *Tonal Analysis: A Schenkerian Perspective*. W. W. Norton & Company, 2018.
Darcy, Warren. *Wagner's Das Rheingold*. Oxford: Oxford University Press, 1993.
Harrison, Daniel. *Pieces of Tradition: An Analysis of Contemporary Tonal Music*. Oxford: Oxford University Press, 2016.
Kirkegaard-Larsen, Thomas Jul. *Analytical Practices in Western Music Theory: A Comparison and Mediation of Schenkerian and Post-Riemannian Traditions*, 288–96 (Ph.D. diss.), Aarhus University, 2020.
McCreless, Patrick. 'Schenker and the Norns', in *Analyzing Opera: Verdi and Wagner*, edited by Carolyn Abbate and Roger Parker, 276–97. Berkeley: University of California Press, 1989.
Wagner, Richard. *The Ring of the Nibelung*, translated and edited by John Deathridge. London: Penguin Books, 2018.

Glossary of Riemannian Symbology

Functions

T⁺ S⁺ D⁺ (or T S D) = Tonic, Subdominant, and Dominant functions (major-mode versions)

°T °S °D = ... (minor-mode versions)

$\bar{T}$ $\bar{S}$ $\bar{D}$ = ... (omitted chord root: e.g., $\bar{D}^7$ in C would be {B,D,F}; {G} is omitted).

[T] [S] [D] = ... (implied functions: e.g., D[Tp]; or, dominant of an implied tonic parallel)

(T) (S) (D) = ... of another function: e.g. (S)Dp = the subdominant of the dominant parallel

𝔻 𝕊 = Dominant of the Dominant; Subdominant of the Subdominant

Transformations

p = Relative transformation: e.g., Tp in C major = A minor

< = Major leading-tone transformation (^8-^7): e.g., 𝔗 in C major = E minor

> = Minor leading-tone transformation (^5-^6): e.g., 𝔓 in F minor = D♭ major

v = Variant transformation (change of mode): e.g., S_v in B♭ major = E♭ minor

NB: p, <, >, v transformations can be, and often are, chained: e.g., $𝔗_v$. Chains of functions are read linearly and cumulatively: e.g., T = C major; 𝔗 = E minor; $𝔗_v$ = E major.

Extensions

⁷ = an 'overtonal seventh'; e.g. C⁷ (C dominant 7th)

ᵛᴵᴵ = an 'undertonal seventh'; or, a minor triad with an under-third: e.g., Sᵛᴵᴵ in G = Cm6/aØ⁷

>ⁿ = a chordal function with a flattened pitch: e.g., C⁻⁹ = C with a flattened 9th

<ⁿ = a chordal function with a sharpened pitch: e.g., B⁻⁵ = B augmented

Schenkerian/Riemannian notations

|O| = Pure function (T S D)

♩ = One transformation applied to a function

⊗ = Two transformations applied to a function

✗ = Three or more transformations applied to a function

Index

Adorno, Theodor 16, 28, 29–30, 52

Beethoven: Piano Sonata in C minor, Op. 10 No. 1 41–44, 50
Benjamin, William 2–3
Bowie, Andrew 3
Brahms: Concerto for Violin and Cello, Op. 102 ('Double Concerto') 44–52, 53–54

Chopin: Op. 28, No. 4 56, 66–68
chromatic music ('free tonality') 1–2, 12
Cohn, Richard: afunctionality of chromatic music 1, 59–60, 64; conflation of tonality with diatonicism 30–31; diatonic(tonal)-chromatic(atonal) binarism 30–31, 60, 62; hexatonic cycles (*see* 'Hexatonicism: Cohnian'); tetrachords 59–62, 64; voice leading as generative 59, 60, 62; Wagner 59
contrapuntal chords 15–17

Dahlhaus, Carl 79
Darcy, Warren 78–79
Douthett, Jack 60–61

enculturated listening 3, 33, 50, 58, 64, 84

function: blended function 10, 11, 65; difference between Riemannian and neo-Riemannian functional theories 11; enrichment (*see* 'contrapuntal chords', 'lunar tonality') 2, 5, 7, 10, 12, 21, 37, 66; harmonic function 1, 3, 11; modulation (of function) 50, 77

Harrison, Daniel 60, 65
Hensel, Fanny: Piano Trio, Op. 11 18–21
hermeneutics: musico-dramatic (in Wagner's *Ring Cycle*) 28–30, 35–37, 74, 83; socio-political (relationship between tonality and society more generally) 7, 9, 26, 37, 52–53, 74, 83–84
hexatonicism 17, 21, 44–50, 53; Cohnian 26, 31, 32–33, 47; tonally situated hexatonicism 33
Hunt, Graham 26–27, 30
Hyer, Brian 1, 3

Kirkegaard-Larsen, Thomas Kul 77
Kurth, Ernst 36

Lambert, Philip 62–63
Lewin, David 27
lunar tonality: functional/tonal fields 41, 43-44; dark-side/light-side functions 33–37, 66, 83–84; general theoretical explanation 32–33, 84; dark-side/light-side functions 33–37, 66, 83–84; in practice 33–37, 41–54, 66–67, 69–71; octatonic submoon function graphs 56, 64–66 (general explanation), 66–71 (in practice)

Index

McCreless, Patrick 74–77
Mickelson, William C. 16

negative dialectics 3–4, 29–30,
  31–32, 36–37, 53, 59, 84
neo-Riemannian theory, NRT (*see
  also* 'Cohn'): afunctionality 1,
  3, 14, 26, 36; atomistic analysis
  in NRT 4; diatonic-chromatic
  binarism 30–31, 36; functional
  relativism 30–31; prolongation
  13–14

octatonic groups/minor third
  relations 14, 77

Rehding, Alexander 7, 9, 13, 14
'Return to Riemann' (why we
  should): 3, 12, 14–15, 16, 28,
  74; diatonic-chromatic synthesis,
  32, 33, 50, 52, 54, 62–63;
  functional prolongation, 79; tonal
  recontextualisation (projection
  of function within chromatic
  music), 31, 33, 37, 49, 51, 54, 64,
  84; treatment of tetrachords (*see
  lunar tonality: octatonic submoon
  function graphs*)
Riemann, Hugo: basics of his theory
  (chord of nature, harmonic series,
  dualism, harmonic proximity)
  7–12; enriched vs enriching
  chords: how to tell the difference
  in highly chromatic music 16, 18;
  Funktionstheorie 9–12; historical
  contexts 7; overdeterminism
  of labelling system 12, 13,
  61–62, 68, 70; overly localised,
  prospective approach 80–81, 83;
  publications 8, 9, 15; reduction
  of extended sonorities to triads
  11–12, 33, 56, 59, 61–62; *Schritt/
  Wechsel* system 9; understanding
  of seventh chords 59, 61

Samson, Jim 30
Schenkerian analysis:
  diatonicisation of
  chromaticism, 50–54; differences
  to Riemann, 54, 77–78; scale-step
  theory, 78
Schenkerian-Riemannian hybrid
  notation: general theoretical
  explanation 75, 79–80; in
  practice 75–77, 79–83; strengths
  80–81, 83
Schubert 1, 31
Smith, Kenneth 14–15, 17

tonality: relationship with tritones
  17–18; Riemannian definition 12
tonicisation & tritone resolution
  17–18
Tonnetz: Riemannian 8–9
totality of tonality 2, 3, 5, 12, 26, 29,
  37, 51, 52–53, 64, 79, 83
transformations (neo-Riemannian):
  13–14, 26, 31, 60

Wagner: *Das Rheingold* 78–79;
  Götterdämmerung 16–17, 26–28,
  33–37, 56, 69–71, 79–83, 80,
  82; Hagen chords 57, 63, 68–71;
  rhetorical dialectics 31, 36,
  56–57, 59, 81; Tarnhelm motif
  27; tonal centricity 79; Valhalla
  motif 27, 28, 29, 33–36, 81; voice
  leading 16

For Product Safety Concerns and Information please contact our EU representative GPSR@taylorandfrancis.com
Taylor & Francis Verlag GmbH, Kaufingerstraße 24, 80331 München, Germany

www.ingramcontent.com/pod-product-compliance
Lightning Source LLC
Chambersburg PA
CBHW051759230426
43670CB00012B/2349